# THE CARING QUESTION

# T·H·E CARING QUESTION

YOU FIRST OR ME FIRST—
CHOOSING A HEALTHY BALANCE

## DONALD A. TUBESING & NANCY LOVING TUBESING

**AUGSBURG** Publishing House • Minneapolis

THE CARING QUESTION

*To our parents*
*Dorothy and Butch*
*Myrt and Karl*
*who shaped our answers to*
*the caring question*

# Contents

# **Acknowledgments**

*Thanks*
to Anita Krause
for lending her expertise on many levels,
including research for Chapter 10

to Mary Boman
for straightforward and caring feedback

to all our friends
who supported us and shared their ideas
along the way, especially the
Duluth Growth for Marriage team

# How to Get the Most Out of This Book

The key to this book's success is you—your insights, observations, and resolutions for restyling your living patterns. Don't just read this book, *use* it! Answer the questions for yourself. Try on the ideas and record your reactions. Feel free to write in the margins, circle, underline, and highlight. Why not start a journal to keep track of the ups and downs of your search for a healthy balance?

We've included several thought-provoking questions at the end of each chapter. You can struggle with these on your own or use them as discussion starters with family or with an established study group. Better yet, gather a group of "neighbors" just for the purpose of sharing and learning together about your individual journeys toward health.

The prescriptions below suggest some creative options for using *The Caring Question* most effectively.

## Rx for Individual Use

*For basic benefit:*

1. Answer for yourself all tests and reflection sheets in each chapter.

*For additional insight:*

2. Scan through each chapter and reread all the italicized questions in the body of the text. On a separate sheet of paper, answer each one.

3. Complete one or more of the "Thought Provokers" found at the end of each chapter.

4. Keep a journal of your ideas, reactions, observations, and insights.

## Rx for Use with Others

*For maximum benefit:*

1. Share your observations and answers from the worksheets in each chapter with your spouse or a special friend.

2. Many of the "Thought Provokers" at the end of each chapter require the participation of another person. Experiment with sharing your insights. Do it around the dinner table, or in the evening with your spouse, your family, or a group of friends.

3. Meet regularly with a group to study and share (an existing group or one you set up just for this purpose).

   • Work through one chapter each session

   • Read the chapter and complete the worksheets individually ahead of time.

   • Use one or more of the "Thought Provokers" as an indepth exercise on the topic during your group study session.

Ultimately the benefit of this book will be determined solely by the assistance it gives you in moving beyond wellness toward personal health-fullness. Please try on our ideas and test them against your life experience. The more you invest, the more you'll gain.

So get out your pencil and get ready to make some notes to yourself. Then read on.

# 1

# The Caring Question
## Love Your Neighbor as Yourself

America is in the midst of a revolution—a revolution called *wellness*.

For years experts have encouraged us to take better care of ourselves for the sake of our health. Now we're finally following their advice—taking to the streets by the thousands, pedaling our bikes, wearing our Nikes, gliding on roller skis, stretching with Simmons, dancing with rock, breakfasting on whole grains, and lunching on lettuce. Hurrah! It's about time we woke up to the need to take care of ourselves. We authors are also part of the renewed cultural awareness of positive health practices—and we applaud it.

We are, however, a bit cautious—concerned with potential excess. Cultural enthusiasm often creates new idols. We believe that positive personal health practices are important, but not enough to sustain well-being. There's simply no staying power in total absorption with self-care—no depth in the shallow self-centered focus that often results in self-worship. Zealots who participate in the wellness revolution to this extreme may inhabit well bodies, but they will not be well people.

We believe that true health-fullness requires investment in people and causes beyond oneself. Healthy people balance their responsibility to reach in and care for themselves and their duty to reach out to others with care and service. Health-full people learn to love both their neighbors and themselves in a healthy balance.

## THE CARING QUESTION

If our time and energy were unlimited, we would easily be able to take care of ourselves and reach out to others as well. Realistically, however, we seldom have enough time to do both—at least not as fully as we might like. The limits of our time and energy force choices on us—tough choices.

Is now the time to take care of me? Or you? When should I say no to you and yes to me? Should I take care of me first or you first? When should I help you fulfill yourself, even at cost to me?

We need to find a healthy balance between caring for self and caring for others. Living in the middle between the two extremes is a delicate balancing act and calls for an endless stream of decisions. Here are some examples.

## DONNA'S DILEMMA

**6:15 p.m.** *Tired, tense, and 30 minutes behind, Donna opens the door and kicks off her shoes. She has just enough time for a well-deserved luxury—a half-hour soak in the tub before the 7:30 Christian Ed meeting. Goodness knows, she needs a little time to herself right* *now, to relax and recover.*

*What's that? The phone!*

"*Hello. . . . Is it possible for me to meet at 6:45 to review the Sunday school curriculum? . . . Yes, it's possible, but. . . .*"

Should Donna say yes to the committee and no to herself, or no to the early meeting and yes to herself?

## FRED'S FIX

**Saturday morning.** *All week Fred looked forward to a 15-mile run with his cronies. Since the marathon was only two weeks away, this would be a test of himself and an important step in training.*

*Why did Judy have to pick now to get upset? he thought. Sure, she'd had a tough time managing this week with two sick kids and her own work as well. Sure company was coming at 6:00. He understood how, with the kids around her feet, the laundry piled high, the shopping undone, and the cleaning neglected, she could feel overwhelmed and irritated that he would take off for a two-hour run, leaving all the responsibility to her.*

*Yes, he wanted to support her and to help out right now. But now was also the time for his long-planned test run with friends.*

Should Fred do as he wants and put Judy on hold? Or should he respond to her feelings and cancel his exercise plans?

## ANSWERING THE CARING QUESTION

If your aging parent requires extensive daily care, how long do you continue to turn your life upside down, and when must you stop and say, "No, I need to care for myself before I fall apart"?

When a friend falls apart and needs emotional support night after night, how much can and should you give? And for how long?

When you've volunteered to work on the church stewardship drive, how many nights should you work before you take one off to be with yourself and your family?

When your boss needs you to work late, should you cancel your plans for the evening or do what you want for yourself?

Dilemmas like this confront us every day—and the choices are tough. How do you answer the caring question? If you always say "You first," you won't be healthy for long. Through plain self-neglect you'll soon wear yourself out in one way or another. If you always say "Me first," your life will be shallow and empty. Self-care is not a deep enough purpose for life. Truly healthy people do something with their wellness, even at cost to themselves.

## STOP AND REFLECT

*Think of a specific instance lately when you sacrificed your own needs to respond to someone else. Would you consider that choice health-full or not? How about an instance when you chose to care for yourself in spite of others' needs. Would you consider that choice health-full?*

*What's the self-care/other-care balance like in your life right now? What percentage of your time and energy are you currently spending on reaching in? On reaching out? Do you consider this balance healthy? Appropriate? Temporary? Will it sustain true health-fullness for you over the long run? Would you like to adjust the balance in any way? How? Estimate for yourself the percentage of times you choose self over others. Others over self. Are you satisfied with that balance?*

## THE HEALTHY BALANCE

If you seek wellness by loving and caring for yourself with no regard for your neighbor, you cannot be whole. If you try loving your neighbor without also loving and caring for yourself, God help your neighbor. Neither of you will be whole. When either target of care, yourself or your neighbor, is neglected, you lose your way on the path to health. Both you and your neighbor need and deserve love in balanced proportions. Full health is possible only when self-care is balanced with service, only when service is offered by one who cares for self.

Our culture sends us conflicting messages, some urging us to "do our duty," others encouraging us to "do what feels good." Both beliefs compete for our attention. It's not easy to maintain a healthy but precarious balance between the two.

How do you carve out a life-style that takes responsibility to others seriously without choosing the life of a self-styled martyr? How do you, on the other hand, achieve personal freedom for self-development without being seduced into the trap of self-worship?

There are no easy formulas for how to remain true to permanent relationships and causes for which you would die on the one hand, and remain responsive to the gratification of your own ever-changing feelings and needs on the other.

To be fully healthy you need to look out for and actively promote the well-being of your family, friends, community, and creation while at the same time attending to the needs of your whole being—body, mind, and spirit. This book is about the process of balancing the two extremes in our search to move beyond well-ness.

## MEASURES OF HEALTH-FULLNESS

We propose four yardsticks for measuring our progress in our search for personal health and vitality.

### Yardstick #1: The Wellness-Movement Criterion: Physical Self-Care

The cornerstone of the movement toward high-level wellness is physical self-care—taking personal responsibility for our well-being. A balanced diet, daily exercise, and freedom from destructive habits typify the healthy life-style. We use the word *wellness* to refer to this concept of optimal physical functioning.

We do in fact have a God-given responsibility to take the very best possible care of our gift of life from our Creator. We believe the road to health begins with the decision to take this responsibility seriously, with a commitment to self-care.

### Yardstick #2: The Wholistic-Health Standard: Whole-Person Self-Care

Our years of involvement in the wholistic health movement have underscored our belief that health (or wholeness) is more than having a body that is trim, agile, and disease-free. From this perspective, well-being is a whole-person affair—involving not only the body, but also the mind, the spirit, and our relationships.

Our responsibility for self-care includes attending to our emotional well-being, to our spiritual vitality, and to the health of our relationships, as well as to our physical needs. According to the whole-person standard, we can be healthy even with our handicaps and limitations.

## Yardstick #3: The Love-Your-Neighbor Principle: Being Well-To-Do

We believe there's more to health than wellness, even whole-person wellness. Healthy people are well-to-*do*. They reach out with a commitment to service and an investment in people and issues beyond themselves. Where they see a need, the healthy reach out to fill it, using their wellness to make a positive difference in their world.

The Christian tradition provides many guidelines and models for such a life of service. Positive action in our "neighborhood" of family, friends, community, and creation enhances our well-being.

## Yardstick #4: The Death-and-Life Factor: Choosing a Healthy Balance

Death is an inevitable fact of life. We believe the appropriate measure of life is not its quantity, but rather its quality; the key question is not how much time we've lived, but how we've spent it. We use the word *health-fullness* to emphasize the fullness of life we enjoy when our life purpose is clearly in focus.

Death is the backdrop against which we see life clearly and find its ultimate meaning. Only when we know clearly the purposes and principles for which we live can we make the choices that lead to a healthy balance of self-care and other-care in our lives. Only then can we move beyond wellness.

## THE SEARCH FOR A HEALTHY BALANCE

Check yourself briefly against these yardsticks. How do you measure up? At which do you excel? Where do you give yourself a moderate or even a low score?

If you found yourself scoring well on Yardsticks #3 and #4 while neglecting self-care (#1 and #2), consider yourself a modern "good Samaritan." Your clarity of purpose and commitment to others is commendable. Part One of *The Caring Question*, "Reaching In," is written especially to help you take better care of the instrument of your service—you!

If you ranked yourself high on Yardsticks #1 and #2 and low on Yardsticks #3 and #4, you'll undoubtedly recognize yourself as firmly grounded in the self-care approach to health. Congratulations! You're halfway to health-fullness. In Part Two of *The Caring Question*, "Reaching Out," you'll find suggestions for some ways to grow in your capacity to love and serve others.

In our pursuit of health-fullness, most of us fall somewhere between these extremes of the good Samaritan style and the self-care style. We feel caught in the middle, trapped between the duty ethic of our parents' generation and the self-fulfillment ethic of the current generation. We're influenced by the values and messages of both—measuring ourselves against the cultural expectation of self-sacrifice while confronted on all sides with the encouragement to "Look out for #1" and "Be all that we can be."

Part Three of *The Caring Question*, "Balance," will help those of us caught in the middle determine when to reach out to others and when to take care of ourselves. It asks the question, "How do you find a healthy balance?"

Let's start by looking at the major principles of positive self-care.

### THOUGHT PROVOKERS

#### For Individual Reflection and Group Discussion

1. Stop for a moment and reflect on the quality of your life. Are you feeling satisfied? Challenged? At

peace? Proud? Energetic? Healthy? Do you have what you want to have? Do you give what you want to give? Overall, would you agree that you have a good life?

Probably your answer is not an unqualified yes or no. We humans are too complicated for easy answers. What are the current signs in your life that indicate yes, your life is rich and full and healthy? What are the current signs in your life that indicate no, your life isn't as health-full as you might wish?

2. Reflect on the balance of reaching in (self-care) and reaching out (other-care) in your life right now. How much of each focus do you include?

- Has the ratio between self-care and other-care changed for you over the years? How?
- What ratio between the two did you see your parents develop? How do/did you feel about that?
- What ratio would you hope your children demonstrate?

# PART 1
## REACHING IN

# 2

# **Keeping Body and Soul Together**
## Creative Self-Care

Most people are *interested* in their health. They generally become *concerned* about it, however, only when some symptom forces them to pay attention—a runny nose, a pain in the chest, an ankle sprain, insomnia, weight gain. Most of us take health for granted until troublesome symptoms "prove" that we are "sick" or "disabled." Then, forced to notice, we pay attention and react to correct the problem. The most effective self-care, however, results from a conscious decision to take care of yourself *before* you get sick.

How do you go about taking care of yourself? In this chapter we'll explore four main ideas that form a foundation for effective day-to-day self-care: (1) health is wholeness; (2) health demands a personal responsibility; (3) health represents a return on your investments; and (4) self-nurture is essential for health-fullness.

## HEALTH IS WHOLENESS

Health is more than having a body that works. Health includes the physical, emotional, intellectual, social, and spiritual dimensions of life, which, when working in harmony, lead to a sense of well-being and satisfaction with life.

The question on a job application that asks you to check whether your health is good, fair, or poor usually refers to the state of your body. Yet both the job applicant and the personnel manager know physical health is profoundly affected by emotions, relationships, and life-style.

Although we usually think about health in physical terms, it really involves all of you—your mind, your connections with people, your sense of hope, your emotions, your satisfaction with work—as well as your body. Health is a multifaceted subject.

Really, we are one single system, a whole. We use many different words to describe sickness and well-being within different components of our life—physical, emotional, social, intellectual, and spiritual—but this is for our own convenience. The words are really verbal fiction. There aren't different forms of sickness or of health. In reality, sickness is a disruption of wholeness in whatever form it occurs, and healing is a return to wholeness. The biblical concept of wholeness includes well-being, health, harmony, and happiness within the single word *shalom*. This word represents God's gifts of wholeness within a person, healing between a person and God, and healthful relationships with all of creation.

There is a unity to the nature of brokenness in its many forms (whether torn ligaments, ruptured vessels, and bone fractures or split personalities, broken hearts, and lives gone to pieces). And there is a unity to the nature of healing in its variety of forms that brings wholeness and new life.

We struggle for wholeness and personal unity against whatever forces tend to wound us, and we heal naturally, by God's grace, through the process of living:

- Our bodies self-correct through internal regulation (homeostasis).
- Our emotions seek peace and acceptance in the face of worry.
- Our intellect uses logic and memory to counteract confusion.
- We respond to our social environment by making up, giving in, speaking up, or fighting back.
- In the face of despair our spirits seek hope, faith, and meaning.

We are always in the process of struggling for an experience of life that tells us with a rush of energy that we are again whole. The synergy of wholeness generates the tingling sense of being fully alive.

To be truly effective, self-care must take seriously our behaviors in every facet of living and not focus only on physical self-care. All of our life-style habits should be examined and judged by whether they create disintegration or wholeness.

## HEALTH IS A PERSONAL RESPONSIBILITY

Self-care is essential. What you do to and for yourself makes a great deal of difference. Take care of your body, your mind, your relationships, and your spirit, and they will return to you a measure of health. Ignore them, or worse, engage in destructive habits, and you will soon pay the price. Let's take physical health as an example.

Current research indicates that physical health over

the life span is as much a result of personal life-style and health habits as it is a matter of good fortune. We're not just victims of bad luck. God does not give heart disease; it's man-made—and now woman-made too! For the first time in the history of the world, a nation, the United States, reported more annual deaths due to overeating than to undereating.

It's our own fault. If we've learned anything in health care in the last 30 years, it's that health doesn't just happen. And sickness doesn't just leap from the woods and grab us; we grow it in our own gardens. Two epidemic killers of the 1980s (heart disease and stroke) are not the result of fate, an ill wind, or a "bug." They are related to life-style. We seldom catch our death of anything anymore; we get it the old-fashioned way: we *earn* it!

All too often we treat ourselves as we treat our cars —mechanically. If nothing is wrong with a car, it's "healthy." If something's not working right, it's "sick." We tend to drive our cars as fast and as far as possible until something breaks. Then we haul it into a shop and say, "fix it." When it's repaired, we get it back on the road and drive it as fast and as far as possible again.

So also with ourselves. Being "healthy" simply means "I am in working order," and I can go about my daily business accomplishing as much as I can as quickly as possible. When something does go wrong, and I can't go on any longer, I haul myself in, shouting, "Fix me, and get me back on the road as soon as possible so I can drive myself like crazy again." Not a very effective long-range plan for either cars or people!

What we've said about physical health is just as true for other aspects of personal self-care. If you want your mind to remain as open and alive at 70 as it was at 20, you'll have to exercise it, encourage its curiosity, and provide it with regular stimulation and challenge. Relationships not cultivated soon wither. They thrive on contact and mutual sharing and support. A spirit undernourished turns cynical and dies. Your spirit needs daily attention. For your whole person to remain vital, you'll have to take responsibility for nourishing all aspects of your health—body, mind, and spirit.

## HEALTH IS A RETURN ON INVESTMENT

Maximum long-term health is most likely to be found in individuals who choose to invest their energies in a health-enhancing life-style. Health-producing habits are the world's best medicine.

Most people regularly pay into a pension plan designed to provide financial security in retirement years. The amount that's put into the plan each day is very small, but over the years it adds up.

Everyone builds a health pension plan. The long-range investments you make in your health accumulate over the years. Viewed on a day-to-day basis, your investment in a nap after lunch, a phone call to a friend, or a five-minute break to watch the sunset doesn't seem to have much long-term effect on your health. That extra cup of coffee, one more rushed hour, another angry argument, or a cynical remark don't seem as if they should detract from your health 20 years from now. But they do. These little bits do add up over the long run.

It's not just the major tragedies and traumas of life that determine your health in the future. Most of those you can't control anyway, so why focus on them? It's the small habits, the daily decisions (just one more cigar, one more time-pressured job, one more deception, one more short night's sleep) that accumulate in your future-health account. Health and sickness are to a large extent the result of daily choices, repeated over the years, to do for ourselves small favors or disfavors.

What about your personal investment plan? Today have you been saving for health or disease? Will your day full of seemingly insignificant behaviors contribute over the long run to wearing you out, or have you been making long-range investments in your future health? Multiplied 10,000 times over the next 30 years, which of your self-care habits would contribute to your health and which would lead toward illness? Check out your Health/Illness Investment Portfolio using the worksheet below.

---

## HEALTH/ILLNESS INVESTMENT PORTFOLIO

What little favors have you done for yourself today that will add up to long-range investments in your health and positive self-care habits? (Examples: leisurely balanced breakfast, walk to work, affirming phone call, three deep breaths.)

_____

_____

_____

_____

Multiplied 10,000 times over the next 30 years, these activities will help immensely in moving you toward your health-investment goals.

Now the other side of the balance sheet. What insults have you offered yourself today that are long-range investments in a future disabling illness? (Examples: three cups of coffee, rushing to meet the bus, shouting at the kids, beer and popcorn at the game.)

_____

_____

_____

_____

Multiplied 10,000 times over the next 30 years, these and other negative self-care habits will probably kill you!

Are there any changes you would like to make?

_____

_____

_____

_____

_____

## SELF-NURTURE IS ESSENTIAL TO HEALTH

To foster positive self-care habits you must be willing to care-fully nurture yourself. An attitude that "I'm worth it" must be cultivated.

Are you beginning to feel uncomfortable with all this focus on you? If so, it's not surprising. Many people are so busy paying attention to the needs of others that they rarely stop long enough to give to themselves. They end up so focused on others that self-nurture is a foreign and even threatening idea.

We're not advocating abandonment of the ideals of service and sacrifice in favor of self-indulgence. The fact remains, however, that self-care is essential for good health.

Even though self-care may feel awkward and faintly sacrilegious, it's certainly the appropriate starting point for promoting your vitality. What would it mean for you to nurture yourself? Feed yourself? Pamper yourself? Take care of yourself? Stand up for yourself? Do you have any idea?

The suggestions below will give you some starters. The next chapters will offer many more. But remember, in personal self-care lack of information is usually not the problem. Good ideas are not enough. Good intentions are not sufficient either. You must be willing to care-fully care for yourself.

## THREE STEPS TO SELF-NURTURE

**Listen to yourself and learn what fills you.** Listening is a gift. You give it to others, you can also give it to yourself. Do you know what fills you? Nurtures you? Feeds you? Listen to your pulse, your feet, your shoulders. Listen to your hopes and your spirit. Listen to your sadness and your joy. If you're hungry for a pizza, a glass of water won't be as satisfying. If you're hungry for some love, shopping probably won't help. If your body is exhausted for lack of exercise, napping isn't the treatment it needs. Listen to yourself. You may need excitement, calm, freedom, laughter, tenderness, serenity.

You could give yourself a lecture or a pat on the back. You could pamper yourself with a gift or a massage. You could go to a movie, read a book, or take a bubble bath. But you can't fill yourself until you know what you need. Ask yourself, "Given all the circumstances in my life right now, what would it mean for me to take better care of myself?" Listen to your answer. Then:

**Take action to care for yourself.** Do something for yourself that fills a need. Don't wait for a miracle or a knight in shining armor. Don't wait for "them"—whoever they are—to notice your need. Stoke your fires yourself, and rekindle your own spirit.

**Set aside time each day for yourself.** Schedule a regular self-care time, even if you start with only five minutes. The regular time will keep you on your own list of needy people and help you focus. You have the right to take care of yourself. Give yourself permission to do so!

## EVALUATE YOUR HABITS

In the next chapters we'll outline specific self-care strategies for promoting physical, mental, relational, and spiritual health. But before you listen to what we have to say about these, please stop and reflect for a moment about your current self-care habits. How well do you take care of yourself in each of the dimensions of life?

The quiz on the next few pages will give you some idea of your current self-care patterns. You may be surprised by some of the questions. "What does laughter have to do with health?" you may ask. What about forgiveness? Seat belts? Or friendships? We'll get to all these issues in later chapters. For now, go ahead and answer the questions.

---

### Health Habit Inventory

| Yes | No | Physical |
|-----|-----|-----|
| ____ | ____ | I participate regularly (three times a week or more) in a vigorous physical-exercise program. |
| ____ | ____ | I eat a well-balanced diet. |
| ____ | ____ | My weight is within 10 lbs. of the ideal weight for my height. |
| ____ | ____ | My alcohol consumption is seven drinks (shot, beer, or glass of wine) or fewer per week. |
| ____ | ____ | I always wear my seat belt. |
| ____ | ____ | I do not smoke cigarettes, cigars, or a pipe. |
| ____ | ____ | I generally get adequate and satisfying sleep. |

### Mental

\_\_\_\_ \_\_\_\_ I seldom experience periods of depression.

\_\_\_\_ \_\_\_\_ I generally face up to problems and cope with change effectively.

\_\_\_\_ \_\_\_\_ I worry very little about future possibilities or things I can't change.

\_\_\_\_ \_\_\_\_ I laugh several times a day and usually fit "play" into my schedule.

\_\_\_\_ \_\_\_\_ I am curious and always on the lookout for new learning.

\_\_\_\_ \_\_\_\_ I maintain a realistic and basically positive self-image.

\_\_\_\_ \_\_\_\_ I choose to feel confident and optimistic.

### Relational

\_\_\_\_ \_\_\_\_ I seek help and support when I need it.

\_\_\_\_ \_\_\_\_ I have at least one friend with whom I can share almost anything.

\_\_\_\_ \_\_\_\_ I have nourishing intimate relationships with family and/or friends.

\_\_\_\_ \_\_\_\_ I experience and express a wide range of emotions and respond to others' feelings appropriately.

\_\_\_\_ \_\_\_\_ Each day includes comfortable and stimulating interaction with others, frequently new acquaintances.

\_\_\_\_ \_\_\_\_ I solicit and accept feedback from others.

\_\_\_\_ \_\_\_\_ I stick up for myself when it's necessary and appropriate.

### Spiritual

\_\_\_\_ \_\_\_\_ I set aside 15-20 minutes each day for prayer or meditation.

\_\_\_\_ \_\_\_\_ I participate in regular spiritual rituals with people who share my beliefs.

\_\_\_\_ \_\_\_\_ I accept my limitations and inadequacies without embarrassment or apology.

\_\_\_\_ \_\_\_\_ I keep the purpose of my life clearly in mind and let it guide my goal setting and decision making.

\_\_\_\_ \_\_\_\_ I regularly offer my time and possessions in service to others.

_____ _____ I am sensitive to ultimate truths and the spiritual dimension of life.

_____ _____ I readily forgive myself and others.

Count up your yes responses for each category and record them below.

| | | |
|---|---|---|
| Physical | _____ | Yes responses |
| Mental | _____ | Yes responses |
| Relational | _____ | Yes responses |
| Spiritual | _____ | Yes responses |
| Total | _____ | Out of 28 questions |

---

## HOW TO INTERPRET YOUR SCORE

Your total of yes responses on the Health Habit Inventory provides a general idea of how well you take care of your health across all dimensions of life. Compare your total score to the Caring Question Standards:

24-28  Excellent: Your habits are enhancing your health.

16-23  Average: You're obviously trying, but there's room for improvement.

Below 16  Poor: The quality of your health is probably diminished by your poor habits.

For specifics on your self-care style, pay particular attention to your score in each of the four categories: physical, mental, relational, and spiritual. If you recorded three or fewer yes responses in any dimension, you're neglecting your health in that area. If you aren't yet experiencing symptoms, you probably soon will. Be sure to read the appropriate self-care chapter and take action to modify your habits.

In those areas where you answered yes four or five times, you're probably taking adequate care of yourself. Your self-care habits do enhance your health, but you might consider upgrading some for optimal health-fullness. There's still room for improvement. Check the corresponding self-care chapter for some new strategies.

Yes responses to six or seven questions in any category indicates that you are practicing positive self-care habits. Congratulations! Over the long run your choices will enhance the quality of your life and your health.

Take a few minutes to reflect on your score and your reactions to it. Use the worksheet below to record your insights and resolutions for change.

---

### Personal Reflection on My Self-Care Patterns

In which areas are your habits an asset?

---

In which areas are your habits a liability?

---

In which areas would you like to make changes?

---

---

Which particular habits would you like to modify?

---

---

---

As you explore your health habit patterns in the next four chapters, rejoice where you've done well and zero in on those aspects of health where you need to boost your self-care investment.

# THOUGHT PROVOKERS

### For Individual Reflection and Group Discussion

1. Where did you get your ideas about what health is? Your models for how to live health-fully? Your training in self-care attitudes and practices?

First, make a list of all the phrases and attitudes about health that you picked up from your parents ("an apple a day," or "put on a hat or you'll catch cold," "keep a stiff upper lip"). Share your list with a friend or someone in your group.

Then brainstorm together all the advertising slogans you can think of that teach something about self-care: ("You deserve a break today," "Plop, plop, fizz, fizz," "When it's time to relax"). What positive or negative self-care message is communicated by each commercial?

2. Based on your present life-style and health habits, what type of health breakdown are you working toward?

_____ Physical illness

_____ Mental fatigue or emotional upheaval

_____ Relationship difficulties

_____ Spiritual emptiness

What kinds of dis-ease are you least likely to suffer because of your positive health habits?

_____ Body      _____ Mind      _____ Relationships

_____ Spirit

3. Read Matthew 14:22-23. In this passage Jesus sends his disciples to the other side of the lake and asks the crowds to leave him alone so he can have some private time and space for renewal and prayer.

- In your life right now, who do you need to get away from?
- What pressures do you need to escape from?

- Where could you go for solitude?
- What do you need once you find that "breathing room"?
- What's stopping you from going right now? (Remember, Jesus did turn his back on the crowd and leave them while they were still clamoring for his attention.)

Share your answers with others in your group. Pay special attention to the variety of "get-away" needs people have and the creative excuses we use to avoid our self-care responsibility.

# 3

# Building the Body Health-Full

## Physical Self-Care

Dear Warren,

It's about time you noticed! So glad my headache finally got to you. I was beginning to think I'd have to zap you with a heart attack before you'd pay attention. Just because I'm not very demanding, that doesn't mean I don't have needs—like sleep. You seem to think my energy reserves are limitless. Better think again. Unless you slow down, I'm going to break down. Do you read me?

Over and out,
Your Body

Dear Chris,

How long has it been since you checked me? Once a month would be appropriate. Breast cancer is the leading cause of death for women in your age group, and early detection usually is lifesaving. I know you were brought up not to "touch" yourself, but this is really important. You're such a caring, giving person, I'd hate to see your life of love and service cut short.

With concern,
Your Torso

Dear Dan,

Ouch! What are you doing to me? Why do I have to carry all your problems around for you? Please let me put them down once in a while!

Your Aching Back

Dear Sally,

The stretching you've been doing is super! I really appreciate it! I'm also delighted you've stopped trying to beat Alice's pace in the pool. You were pushing me too hard for a while. Just because exercise is good for me doesn't mean that *more* or *harder* exercise is better.

Thanks for listening,
Your Body

Dear George,

Do me a favor, please. Keep track for the next month of all the booze you drink. Every drop. Then come back with a plan for changing that, before I'm totally incapacitated.

Sincerely,
Your Liver

How about you? How does your body feel about how you've been treating it lately? If your body could write you a letter, what would it say?

Stop for a minute and grade yourself on the way you've taken care of your body *this past week*. Give yourself a separate grade for both effort and achievement.

|  | Effort | Achievement |
|---|---|---|
| What I've put into my body (eating, drinking, smoking) | _____ | _____ |
| What I've done to it (pace, workload, pressure) | _____ | _____ |
| What I've done with it (exercise) | _____ | _____ |
| How I've let it rest (sleep, relaxation) | _____ | _____ |

# WAKING UP TO YOUR BODY

As we were growing up, most of us took our physical health for granted. Unless we had physical limitations or we became sick and couldn't go on, we never thought much about our health. Our parents took responsibility for trying to ensure a relatively healthy diet and sleep pattern. They may even have supported or insisted on regular exercise. They took us in for checkups, made sure our immunizations were up to date, kissed our minor pains away, and worried when appetites waned or cheeks flushed.

Most of us absorbed some of these physical-health-care principles and incorporated them into our lifestyle but never consciously accepted responsibility for our own health promotion. We more likely shifted the responsibility to a spouse, to our physician, or to fate. Fortunately, some of us learn good self-care health habits anyway. Too many of us don't. We smoke. We drink. We eat too much of the wrong things. We experiment with drugs. We're careless about safety precautions. We're too busy to exercise. We don't pay attention to early warning signals. Or we spend too much time worrying about every twinge and ache.

As long as our life is free from pain or disease, as long as we're able to function as we wish and have adequate energy, we're not likely to worry too much about our physical health until our bodies let us down. You get mono or herpes. You slip a disc or break your wrist. Your hay fever blossoms. Your appendix ruptures. A physical exam reveals hypertension or a hernia. Your cramps seem unbearable. That nagging headache won't go away. You can't sleep. A motorcycle accident lands you in the hospital with a crushed hip. Toxic shock syndrome threatens your life and your childbearing.

Suddenly physical health-fullness becomes an important issue for you, perhaps a life-and-death issue. When your body starts writing nasty, painful letters, you're more inclined to take it seriously, aware both of its vulnerability and its resiliency. Whether it comes through illness or accident or a health class, this kind of awareness usually marks the beginning of responsible self-care.

## BUILDING SELF-CARE HABITS

Health care is something you do every day. It's not something to be delivered—it's to be acted out. It's easy to take your body for granted and not realize you are paying a price. What you do for yourself over the years has a tremendous impact on how you feel physically and how you feel about yourself.

Up to about 25 years of age your body increases in energy and strength. It's remarkable the amount of reserve a 20-year-old body has in the bank. From about 25 on you start a long slide, as your energy reserves and strength decline. But you don't notice it right away. Somewhere in the middle or late 40s, people suddenly realize that they are increasingly becoming a maintenance problem. It's then that the results of your self-care habits over the years start to show clearly.

## THE LONG AND THE SHORT OF IT

Ours is the first generation possessing the knowledge and technology that enables us to deliberately increase our life span by health-behavior choices. We know that buckling up for safety as we drive can increase the odds for adding years to our life. We're bombarded with information about the life-shortening effects of smoking cigarettes. We know that if we exercise regularly and scrutinize our diets we can minimize the risk of strokes and heart attacks.

We may even receive a computer printout of our health risks and life expectancy along with an annual physical exam. Long life is certainly one goal of physical health care. We all want to die as old as possible, feeling as young as possible, perhaps with as little pain as possible.

Physical well-being is also important to us in the short run. You could characterize health-fullness as the capacity to function as you wish, adequate energy to go through your day without physical fatigue, strength to meet the challenges you encounter, and endurance to maintain your desired pace. Your standards for well-being may differ greatly from your neighbor's: she may need the strength to climb a telephone pole, while you need only carry a briefcase.

When it comes right down to it, the specifics of a physical self-care plan are highly personal. It's your body and your life. You know what you want from and for yourself and what you're willing to invest or sacrifice.

We believe there are four major areas that you ought to consider in your physical-self-care plan: exercise, relaxation, nutrition, and chemical use. Each area has both long- and short-range costs and benefits in relation to endurance, energy, strength, and personal limitations.


## EXERCISE: BUILDING YOUR STAMINA

Americans are exercising in ever-increasing numbers. Designer running shoes are fast becoming the status symbol of the 1980s. People exercise for weight control, for strength, for endurance, for cardiovascular fitness, for the camaraderie and challenge of a sport, for peace of mind, even to keep up with the Joneses. Most of us know that "exercise is good for you" but are only vaguely aware of "how much" or "which kind" or "for what purpose."

Physical fitness experts suggest that all of us should be able to lift our own body weight using only our arms and shoulders. If you can't do a chin-up, exercises to strengthen your upper body would seem appropriate. If a trim physical appearance is important to your sense of well-being, calisthenics and tummy tighteners are in order.

However, if maximum health-fullness is your goal, aerobic exercise is the choice. Moderate exercise (just 20 minutes at a time) on a regular basis (three times a week) will help you increase the capacity of your lungs, strengthen your heart, and develop muscular efficiency. This development of your heart–lung capacity (called cardiovascular fitness) improves circulation so that your body receives more nutrients and oxygen while efficiently ridding itself of wastes. Your enzyme system stays balanced, your muscles can relax more completely, you fall asleep more easily, and your endurance increases. Physical fitness experts judge your cardiovascular fitness as adequate when you can run 1½ miles in 12 minutes or carry on a conversation easily while exercising. Obviously, as you get older, brisk walking may become more appropriate than running.

People who exercise regularly report other benefits, including good muscle tone, a general feeling of well-being, relief from depression, tension release, and weight control. Paradoxical as it sounds, you will probably have far more energy following exercise than you did before. Our bodies seem to thrive on regular exercise. When you feel down and tired, you may need to exercise rather than relax.

*What about you? How do you feel about your current level of physical activity? Are you exercising on a regular basis? Does your routine include aerobic conditioning? Do you have any limitations that prevent regular exercise? What changes in your exercise habits might enhance your health-fullness?*

The seven strategies for building your stamina listed below outline a commonsense approach to aerobic exercise.

## SEVEN STAMINA BUILDERS

**Check your attitude.** Ask yourself whether you are willing to exercise at least every other day. If you aren't, then you should not exercise at all. Irregular exertion for which your body isn't prepared does more harm than good. Old joke: if you want to know when you will die, be a weekend athlete; you'll probably die on a weekend.

**Design an aerobic program that makes sense for you.** Almost any exercise that makes your heart work hard will suffice: walking, swimming, cross-country skiing, tennis, jumping rope, climbing stairs, calisthenics, dancing, etc. Do what you most enjoy. The key is steady exercise that keeps your heartbeat elevated for at least 20 minutes three times a week. The chart below describes the "target pulse rate" aerobic exercise method.

### Target Pulse Rate

Activities involving prolonged use of large-muscle groups are dependent upon the ability to deliver oxygen to the working muscles. Repeated muscular contractions rely on aerobic (oxygen-using) chemical reactions. Certain training principles should be followed to develop aerobic

47

endurance. Exercise should be performed a *minimum of three days per week* but not more than five days per week. Each exercise session should involve a *minimum of 15 minutes* of exercise at a work intensity sufficient to bring about a heart rate of at least *60 percent of your maximal heart-rate reserve*. The types of activities are numerous. Activity should involve repeated rhythmical movements of large-muscle groups in a continuous fashion. Sample activities include walking, swimming, jogging, cycling, cross-country skiing, running, skating, hiking, and rope skipping. Additionally, once a certain level of fitness is reached, endurance game activities (racquetball, handball, squash, tennis, badminton, or basketball) may be of benefit in maintaining cardiorespiratory fitness.

The following guide can be used by persons who are relatively healthy, or by those who have been cleared by their physician, for estimation of a target heart rate for training. *If you are over the age of 35 or suspect you may not be capable of exercising, you should consult your personal physician prior to beginning a new exercise program.*

## A GUIDE FOR ESTABLISHING TARGET HEART RATES IN HEALTHY ADULTS

| Age in Years | Estimated Maximal Heart Rate | Heart Rate Standing at Rest | | | | |
|---|---|---|---|---|---|---|
| | | 50 | 60 | 70 | 80 | 90 |
| 20-25 | 200 | 125 | 130 | 135 | 140 | 145 |
| 30 | 190 | 122 | 128 | 132 | 138 | 142 |
| 35°° | 185 | 120 | 125 | 130 | 135 | 140 |
| 40°° | 180 | 118 | 122 | 128 | 132 | 138 |
| 45°° | 175 | 115 | 120 | 125 | 130 | 135 |
| 50°° | 170 | 112 | 118 | 122 | 128 | 132 |
| 55°° | 165 | 110 | 115 | 120 | 125 | 130 |
| 60°° | 160 | 108 | 112 | 118 | 122 | 128 |
| 65°° | 155 | 105 | 110 | 115 | 120 | 125 |
| 70°° | 150 | 102 | 108 | 112 | 118 | 122 |

°°Persons over 35 should consult their physicians prior to beginning an exercise program.

To check your heart rate while exercising, stop exercising and count the number of beats that occur in 10 seconds. Then multiply by six. If you are over your target heart rate, slow down; you're working too hard. If you are under the target heart rate, increase your intensity. On warm days, especially early in the session, decrease your activity level or wait until evening to exercise.

Source: "Recommended Quantity and Quality of Exercise for Developing Physical Fitness in Healthy Adults," American College of Sports Medicine Position Statement, *Medicine and Science in Sports* 10(3): 1978.

**Start slowly and build gradually.** Don't push yourself too hard. Increase your capacity over a year, not over a week or two. Know your own limits. Start by stretching and exerting lightly. Then don't push yourself too hard, even after you're fit. If you feel tired rather than energized one hour after exercise, then you've probably done too much. Cut back for a while. If you're training to be healthy, exercise should never hurt.

**Always spend five to ten minutes warming up before exercising and cooling down afterwards.** Give your body a chance to get ready for the pace and to recover from the exertion. It's tempting to skip these steps when you're pressed for time. Don't give in! That's when you need the transition most. Systematically stretch each muscle every day. We're only beginning to learn the importance of stretching both as an adjunct to exercise and as an intrinsically healthy activity.

**Build supports and rewards into your program.** Start an exercise chart with daily gold stars and periodic rewards for persistence. Treat yourself to a movie after a week or a new swimsuit after a month. Notch your miles on a walking stick or a pedometer. Add music to your routine. Exercising with friends or family may provide mutual encouragement as well as relief from boredom. If you don't like exercising alone, find ways to combat the loneliness of the long-distance runner.

**Combine exercise goals.** If looking fit and trim is important to you, add exercises to tone and shape the body (sit-ups, push-ups, leg lifts, weights) to your aerobic routine. Yoga postures provide physical conditioning that helps maintain flexibility and decrease muscular tension.

**Exercise up to your limitations.** With an ounce of precaution and a pound of creativity, those of us with physical limitations can devise an aerobic exercise program. If you are over 35 or have any serious illness, especially heart problems, consult your physician before exercising. Walking may be the best starting point for you, and it's an excellent exercise for anyone.

When you exercise regularly, you'll look and feel better and will be able to ward off the negative effects of distress more effectively. After you're into it, regular exercise acts as a stimulant. It's a healthy high, a positive addiction. Physical fitness may not add years to your life, but it will add life to your years. Prevent rust and rot—exercise!


## A NOTE TO NONBELIEVERS

If your exercise these days has been limited to climbing walls, dragging your heels, flying off the handle, or running around in circles, you're probably feeling guilty with all this focus on aerobics. Good! Keep on feeling that way until it's so uncomfortable that you do something about it. Then come back to this chapter and plan an exercise program that meets your needs and fits your life-style. Exercise fanatics can be tough to live with. When you do decide to start exercising, choose an activity and pace that's right for *you*—and avoid making comparisons.

# RELAXATION: SHORT-CIRCUITING THE
# STRESS CONNECTION

Stress is one of the most pervasive and intriguing health problems of our times. The stress response is a marvelous mind/body mechanism that gears us up to meet dangerous situations with an extra burst of energy. Unfortunately, we tend to abuse this resource by calling on it too often—overloading our schedules, overreacting to people and life events, overburdening ourselves with worries or expectations. We run the danger flag up too often. It's as if you shift into passing gear to get out of a tight spot and then have trouble gearing down. When you push yourself at high speed all the time, you're likely to run out of gas more quickly, and you lose your emergency acceleration power.

Stress seems to have a similar effect on our bodies. Many of us suffer the side effects of chronic stress—unresolved muscle tension, elevated blood pressure, increased heartbeat, general arousal. We don't know how to get out of passing gear. Eventually the tension, arousal, and tightness seem normal, and we find ourselves more vulnerable to illness and poor self-care habits. Chronic tension can lead to knotted muscles, lower mobility, degenerative joint and spine problems, and exhaustion.

Systematic relaxation reverses the emergency stress response by decreasing unconscious muscular tension and regulating breathing. Since most people don't really know how to relax, the process takes practice and persistence.

You can relax in a hundred different ways. Each method is, of course, somewhat different from the others, but each is based on the same principle. By exercising your powers of consciousness, you can control most, if not all, of your physiological processes, including your heartbeat and blood pressure. By using any of the popular relaxation methods, you can learn to release tension and thereby control your stress.

There are many good books about stress and relaxation you can consult for specifics. We recommend *Stress/Unstress* by Dr. Keith W. Sehnert (Augsburg, 1981) and our own book *Kicking Your Stress Habits* (Signet, 1981). Our purpose here is just to raise your consciousness about the role of stress in your healthfullness and the potential for regular relaxation in your self-care program.

*What about you? In what ways do you normally relax? How often and when? Is your present style efficient and effective for you? What recommendation would you make to yourself about even more healthfull patterns?*

If you choose tension-reduction as one of your routes to fuller health, the five roads to relaxation described below will give you some direction. Remember, for relaxation to help, you must do it. Knowing that you could relax if you wanted to won't get you the results you need. Self-care for chronic tension begins with letting go. Make deep relaxation one of your daily habits!

## FIVE ROADS TO RELAXATION

**Use any one method of relaxation each day for one month.** Practice the approach you select for at least 20 minutes each day. At the end of the month evaluate the impact of your program on your sense of well-being and vitality.

**Systematically check your physical tension level.** Then consciously relax the muscles where you find tension. Here's how. Stretch each muscle, then release the tension. Notice which muscles you have been holding tight. Test your whole body, one part at a time. Check your hands, wrists, forearms, upper arms, shoulders, neck, face, jaw, chest, back, groin, stomach, thighs, calves, ankles, feet, and toes. Where do you hold tension? Once you're aware of your favorite storage places, you can check your tension level throughout the day by focusing on these spots.

**Periodically relax your favorite tension spots.** To relax a particular tension area, tighten the muscles, then let go fully; repeat three times. Or imagine as you breathe in that you're inflating the tight muscle; when you breathe out imagine the muscle deflating. Or meditate on relaxing the muscle until you can feel your pulse in it.

**Take "yawn and belly-breathing breaks," at least three every hour.** Stand and stretch, then open your mouth and the back of your throat. Stretch until a yawn catches and carries you for a moment. If you're too tight, you can't yawn. Keep at this until you can yawn. A yawn is total tension, then complete relaxation. It's effective, and it feels good.

**Clear your mind and prepare for sleep.** Focus on relaxing at the end of each day. Don't rehash the whole day's troubles right up until bedtime. You need some time away from the pressure. If you've struggled with a problem all day, at night you need to let go. Give up the problems of the day to God and let go! The key is that you must be *willing* to slack off.

Sometimes a long walk or vigorous exercise helps. Giving and/or receiving a massage, taking a warm bath, and drinking a bedtime glass of milk can all be effective late-evening relaxants.

Develop the expectation that sleep will allow peace and strength to creep back into your pores and joints. Envision this healing action taking place.

# NUTRITION: BUILDING STRONG BODIES
# EIGHT WAYS

Nutritional self-care focuses on two habit patterns—
*what* you eat (the content) and *how* you eat (the
process). Let's take a look at content of your diet first.

*Think back to yesterday and see if you can remem-*
*ber everything you ingested during the day: breakfast,*
*coffee break, lunch, after-school snack, snitches during*
*supper preparation, after-work cocktails, supper, late*
*night snacks, a nightcap. How many calories would*
*you estimate you took in yesterday?*

Check the Caloric Intake Chart on page 55 to find
the recommended calorie intake for a person of your
age/height/sex. If you took in more than you needed,
and maintain that pattern, you'll gain weight unless
you exercise to expend the extra calories. If you took
in less than you needed, and maintain that pattern,
you'll lose weight and will lose more if you also exercise. That's all there is to weight control. If you're
within 10 pounds of the recommended standard
weight for your height, your calorie intake is probably
just about right.

But nutrition means more than weight control. Food
is more than calories. We eat not only to satisfy our
hunger, but to provide our body with the nutrients it
needs to maintain health-fullness. Our body needs fuel
(proteins) to repair itself and "regulators" (vitamins,
minerals, and fiber) to keep our systems in balance.
Go back to your list of calories for yesterday. How
much of what you ate was empty calories (sugar, junk
food, alcohol, soda)? If the percentage is over 10,
you're flirting with danger over the long run. The remaining 90 percent (or 60 percent or 50 percent) of
your calories has to provide all of the 55 nutrients your
body needs to stay healthy. No wonder Orson Welles

# MEAN WEIGHTS AND HEIGHTS AND RECOMMENDED CALORIC INTAKE*

| Category | Age (Years) | Weight (Pounds) | Height (Inches) | Energy needs (with range in calories) |
|---|---|---|---|---|
| MALES | 11-14 | 99 | 62 | 2700 (2000-3700) |
| | 15-18 | 145 | 69 | 2800 (2100-3900) |
| | 19-22 | 154 | 70 | 2900 (2500-3300) |
| | 23-50 | 154 | 70 | 2700 (2300-3100) |
| | 51-75 | 154 | 70 | 2400 (2000-2800) |
| | 76+ | 154 | 70 | 2050 (1650-2450) |
| FEMALES | 11-14 | 101 | 62 | 2200 (1500-3000) |
| | 15-18 | 120 | 64 | 2100 (1200-3000) |
| | 19-22 | 120 | 64 | 2100 (1700-2500) |
| | 23-50 | 120 | 64 | 2000 (1600-2400) |
| | 51-75 | 120 | 64 | 1800 (1400-2200) |
| | 76+ | 120 | 64 | 1600 (1200-2000) |
| PREGNANCY | | | | +300 |
| LACTATION | | | | +500 |

*From *Recommended Dietary Allowances*, revised 1979. Food and Nutrition Board, National Academy of Sciences-National Research Council, Washington, D.C.

The information in this table has been assembled from data of the Department of Health, Education and Welfare/National Center for Health Statistics. The customary range of daily energy output for adults, shown in parentheses, is based on a variation of plus or minus 400 calories at any one age. Youngsters' ranges vary more widely because of growth needs.

55

quipped, "One-third of what we eat keeps us alive. The other two-thirds keeps our doctors alive!"

Six of the ten leading causes of death in the United States have been linked to diet. It makes good sense to develop our eating skills so that we can make smart choices. Most of us aren't experts in nutrition, but then neither are most physicians or nurses. We recommend *Jane Brody's Nutrition Book* (Bantam, 1982) as one of the most complete sources of accurate information on nutritional self-care.

Although nutrition may seem complicated, you don't need to be a chemist or dietitian to improve your eating patterns. Mostly you need common sense, and a few basic principles.

## FIVE FOOD FUNDAMENTALS

**Keep your weight normal.** Be calorie wise. Eat only as much food as your body uses. Cut down on portion sizes rather than cutting out food. Remember, calories in alcohol count too! One drink (100 calories) is five percent of a 2000 calorie diet.

**Eat more fruits, vegetables, starches.** Our ancestors stayed trim on bread, potatoes, and beans. These unrefined carbohydrates also provide valuable protein, iron, trace minerals, and fiber.

**Cut down on sugar and sweets.** Sugar accounts for one-fourth of the calories in most Americans' diets. Corn syrup, fructose, dextrose, raw sugar, brown sugar, and turbinado sugar are all still sugar! Sugar calories slide down too easily, too quickly—up to 600 calories per minute.

**Eat less fat and cholesterol.** All kinds of fats seem to lead to heart disease. Choose lean cuts; trim fat before cooking; bake, broil, or boil. Avoid prepared meats;

substitute legumes; avoid spreads and dressings. Cut out rich desserts. Use low-fat milk products.

**Reduce salt intake.** Excess salt is linked to high blood pressure. Season creatively with lemon, onion, garlic, wine, herbs, spices. Convenience foods are loaded with salt and other sodium compounds. Avoid processed foods. Cut recipe portion of salt to one-half or less.

## CHANGING EATING HABITS

Eating is one of the primary ways we receive nurturing. When you were very small, you probably got lots of warmth and cuddling and love talk and affirmation along with the milk. Some of us still look forward to mealtime as an opportunity to fill ourselves up emotionally as well as physically. That can cause problems! It's also likely that some lifelong eating habits got started when you were a youngster. Did you dawdle around at feeding time or gulp and run? Were you deprived of food when you were hungry, or forced to eat more than you desired, or encouraged to eat at your own pace? Were mealtimes intimate moments in your family or arenas for conflict?

Stop for a minute and take an inventory of your eating habits from the process viewpoint.

---

### Eating Habits Inventory

*Usually Sometimes Never*

1. Do you tend to eat in response to anxiety, tension, or depression? \_\_\_\_ \_\_\_\_ \_\_\_\_

2. Do you eat at the same time as you participate in other activities, such as reading, watching TV, cooking? \_\_\_\_ \_\_\_\_ \_\_\_\_

3. Do you use eating as your primary mode of celebration?     \_\_\_\_     \_\_\_\_     \_\_\_\_

4. Do you use eating as your primary mode of grieving?     \_\_\_\_     \_\_\_\_     \_\_\_\_

5. Do you eat quickly from the beginning of the meal to the end?     \_\_\_\_     \_\_\_\_     \_\_\_\_

6. Is a clean plate, rather than a full feeling, your cue that you are done eating?     \_\_\_\_     \_\_\_\_     \_\_\_\_

7. Are you easily stimulated to eat by TV advertisements, billboards, magazine pictures?     \_\_\_\_     \_\_\_\_     \_\_\_\_

8. Do you enjoy discussing food?     \_\_\_\_     \_\_\_\_     \_\_\_\_

9. Do you feel compelled to eat food that is offered by others so they won't be offended?     \_\_\_\_     \_\_\_\_     \_\_\_\_

10. Do you binge and then feel guilty?     \_\_\_\_     \_\_\_\_     \_\_\_\_

---

If you answered *usually* to more than one of these questions, you may be using food in an addictive pattern. Overeating is a learned addiction. You're probably more sensitive to the smell of food and to TV ads. Foodaholics eat when they're hungry—and when they're tired, bored, angry, depressed, celebrating, or socializing. If eating satisfies more than physical hunger for you, your self-care habits will need to include learning how to identify your hungers and how to satisfy at least some of them with other kinds of nourishment, like stimulation or laughter or enriching conversation.

*What about you? How do you feel about the way you nurture your body and your eating style? Is there anything you would like to change to enhance your health-fullness?*

Before leaving the issue of physical self-care, especially as related to nutrition and nurture, we need to take a look at one other area of health habits—the use of alcohol, drugs, and other substances that alter our consciousness and impair our health-fullness.

## THE HIDDEN COSTS OF CHEMICALS

Have you used any drugs today? No? What about caffeine (in cola, coffee, tea, cocoa, chocolate)? Tobacco? Aspirin? Other over-the-counter or prescription drugs? Marijuana? Alcohol?

We are a "feel-good" society. Bombarded with messages that tell us we should not be tired, tense, depressed, or in pain, we turn to chemicals, stimulants, and drugs to ease our pain. Covering up our discomfort can be a costly choice. When we override our personal biofeedback mechanism, we lose touch with our own internal wisdom about health-fullness and short-circuit our early-warning system that may be signaling a potential problem.

Smoking is another expensive pleasure. The price is emphysema, chronic bronchitis, lung cancer, heart disease. Not now, maybe not five years from now, but someday you'll pay the price. Tobacco companies have spent billions of dollars trying to link smoking to the beautiful things in life. In real life smoking is linked only to disability and death.

The use of chemicals, just like food, can be addicting. Caffeine is the most widely used mood-altering drug in America. Do your six cups of coffee or four

Cokes a day represent an addiction? Research indicates that an ounce of alcohol daily may be health-full. Is your wine before bed or beer after work relaxing or addicting? Or both? Alcohol is still the most abused drug in our culture. Valium is the most overprescribed.

Alcohol, over-the-counter medications, prescription medications, caffeine, and tobacco all have their place in our society. Which chemicals do you use regularly? How do you feel about this quantity and pattern of use? You alone know whether you should slow down or stop your use of one or a number of these substances.

The question is, how does your use and/or abuse of chemicals affect your overall health? What positive effect would you expect if you changed that pattern?

## PROMOTING FAN MAIL

Careful attention to the four areas of physical self-care—exercise, relaxation, nutrition, and chemical use—will allow your body to give you the energy you need to do the things you want in life for yourself and for others. Want to receive a love letter from your body? Give it the care you would give a lover. Love it gently. Love it daily.

Dear Self,
    Thanks for listening to my needs!
                    Love,
                    Your Body

## REFLECTIONS

Before we move on to consider mental self-care, please stop and reflect on your overall physical-self-care habits. Do they enhance or erode your health-fullness?

## Personal Reflection on My Physical Health

My exercise patterns (type of exercise, regularity, intensity, current physical condition)

_____

_____

My relaxation patterns (stress, methods, preparation for sleep)

_____

_____

My eating patterns (weight, nutrition, eating style)

_____

_____

My chemical-use patterns (caffeine, alcohol, smoking, other)

_____

_____

## Wish List for Physical Health-Fullness

List here everything you can imagine wanting for your physical health-fullness. What would you like to be able to *do?* To *know?* To *feel?* To *stop?* Let your imagination run free. Don't limit yourself in any way. The wishes don't have to be practical. Have fun dreaming.

I wish I could:

_____

_____

_____

_____

## THOUGHT PROVOKERS

### For Individual Reflection and Group Discussion

1. Few people are satisfied with their reflections in a mirror. Although we know "God doesn't make no junk,"

most of us still wonder if God didn't piece us together out of the spare-parts bin.

As you take inventory of yourself as a physical specimen, which parts seem to be high-quality, factory originals? Your beautiful eyelashes or bulging biceps? Which seem to be inferior-quality, ill-fitting spare parts? Your problem kidney or heavy thighs?

Draw a picture of your body. Spend some time embellishing your drawing. Highlight the weak parts or trouble spots, the vulnerable areas you try to hide or protect. Then use another color or different symbols to present your glories and strong points as well.

Now draw a picture of the physical ideal you would like to reach with proper self-care. What kind of body are you dreaming about? What do you want to be able to do with it? To have it do for you? What changes will you have to make in order to reach these goals?

Share your pictures and insights with someone in your family or with your group.

2. Where in your body do you usually store tension? What situations tend to make you most tense? Reflect briefly on your relaxation patterns.

- What activities help you relax?
- What memories or mental images bring you peace and tranquility?
- Are there any special places where you feel particularly calm?
- What music helps soothe you?

How often do you take advantage of these tension tamers?

3. Write a letter from your body to yourself. Take a whole page or two. Let your body say all it wants you to hear. Start by writing: "Dear [your name]." Then get the ball rolling. What does your body want to say

about how you exercise it, what you feed it, how you let it rest, the poisons with which you pollute it?

Read your letters out loud and discuss them together as a group.

# 4

# A Better Idea
## Mental Self-Care

From the whole-person perspective, the second natural focus for self-care is mental health-fullness. Unfortunately mental health has a bad name in our culture, calling up images of craziness, behavioral problems, and emotional outbursts. Another fine example of illness masquerading as health!

The medical profession has tried to help us understand the mind-body connection, but unfortunately the label psychosomatic (mind-body) illness is all too frequently interpreted as a putdown, a judgment of weakness rather than an affirmation of the miraculous mystery and powerful potential of our minds. Too bad we don't talk more often about psychosomatic *health!*

## WHAT IS MENTAL HEALTH?

Mental health is more than "nerves" or avoiding "the crazies" or illness that's "all in your head" or a "figment of your imagination." Mental health encompasses our mechanisms for taking in and interpreting our environment at the level of fact and feeling. It includes our thinking processes, our capacity to experience feelings, and our sense of self-worth.

Mental health refers to the health-fullness of your *thinking*—the limberness of your mind, your logic patterns, your problem-solving skills, your sense of humor, your curiosity, your process for labeling and organizing your life experience.

In meeting the daily demands of life, mentally healthy people try to cope with problems as they arise, accept responsibility, welcome new experiences and new ideas, use their natural capacities, think for themselves and make their own decisions, put forth their best efforts, and find this satisfying.

*Emotional* health-fullness is a second component of mental health: your capacity to feel deeply, your sensitivity to feelings, your willingness to experience feelings, your motivations, the appropriateness of your responses and your intuition. This sketches a picture of one who can usually cope with emotions—fear, anger, love, jealousy, guilt, or worry—and take life's disappointments in stride.

*Self-respect* is the third ingredient for mental well-being—your level of self-awareness, your attitude toward your strengths and limitations, your internal standards. Mentally healthy people know themselves and feel comfortable with themselves and others. They exhibit a confidence and trust in their capacity to deal with whatever situation comes along.

Does all this sound a bit heavy? Who could be all of this all of the time? No one! No one has all the characteristics of good mental health all of the time. Everyone experiences disappointments and fears, anxiety and doubt, ups and downs. Mental health does not mean perfection. Instead it reflects a willingness to

65

live life openly and fully, acknowledging your limitations and affirming your strengths.

*What about you? How would you rank your mental health? Do you feel in control of yourself? Can you laugh easily? Do you laugh each day? Can you cry easily? When was the last time? Give yourself a grade for common sense. How about your mental alertness and curiosity? What did you learn yesterday? How about today?*

Mental health requires the capacity to think clearly, the willingness to experience your feelings fully, and the esteem to trust yourself. Let's look at each of these dimensions more closely and pinpoint some strategies for health-full self-care.

## EXPLORING YOUR INTELLECT

Daily life requires us to process and retain enormous quantities of information. Fortunately the brain is a storage and retrieval system many times more complicated and efficient than the most complex computer. Remembering phone numbers, keeping appointments in mind, planning menus, listening to your children—all routine tasks, but tasks that require substantial mental alertness. Figuring your income tax, tailoring a suit, driving a car, and giving a speech demand a bit more concentration. Our minds allow us to absorb and sort and process hundreds of thousands of bits of data each day, which we then combine in the correct way to tie our shoes or read a street sign or unlock our bicycle.

Scientists are beginning to find evidence that this computerlike, logical connection of images, ideas, and instructions is primarily the function of the left hemisphere of the brain. The right hemisphere seems to be more in charge of combining information in new ways. We call this process creativity. Although we may not be able to create an Adam out of dust, we spark of divinity when we mix and synthesize and combine bits and pieces of our world, recasting them into some form that's new—at least for us. We come up with a novel idea or give old ideas a new twist. We intuit the connections between events or people. We solve problems. We daydream. We see the incongruity around us and laugh.

*How creative are you in seeing new options? How good is your memory? How curious are you? How active is your imagination and fantasy? How well do you concentrate? How humorous or clever are you? How well do you make judgments?*

The answers to these questions are qualitative, not quantitative. They're relative to your personal capacities and limitations. An IQ of 130 doesn't insure mental health. Nor does one of 80 preclude creativity. There is no absolute standard or final destination. Learning is a lifelong process of absorbing and forgetting, relearning and remembering, focusing and drifting, connecting and disconnecting and reconnecting. The assumption that we peak mentally at 18 is absurd!

## FOUR STEPS TO A LIVELY MIND

**Keep your thinking cap on.** A public-service announcement in our area reminds us that a mind is a horrible thing to waste. Our minds need to be nourished just like our bodies. Read books. Ask questions. Explore. Experiment and grasp every opportunity to "fill'er up!"

**Accept and meet new challenges willingly.** Every problem is a challenge turned inside out. Every change can become stimulating as you seek to find ways to adjust. Be curious. Seek out new information. Challenge yourself to make tough decisions from which you will learn. Changing jobs, accepting new responsibilities, writing an article or speech, or taking a course can be an adventure—if you make it one.

**Control your energy output.** When you're overburdened, it's important to start limiting your investments. Choose to say no to some possibilities. Say it before you're empty, while you still have some reserve in your tank. Save some of your energy for yourself. When you're bored or underburdened, say yes! Seek out a new commitment, cause, or friendship.

**Cultivate creativity.** Stretch your imagination. Take a new route to church. Make up a story. State your problem in 10 different ways. Ask open-ended questions. Try a new recipe, or an old recipe with a new ingredient. Look for alternatives. Exaggerate your dilemma. Rearrange your office or your junk drawer or your priorities. Watch for the incongruities—and laugh! You can double your energy when you add a creative twist.

## INVESTIGATING YOUR EMOTIONS

Mental health is characterized by a wide variety of clear, strong feelings at all points of the compass: irritation, anger, rage, excitement, anxiety, worry; despair, sadness, disappointment; joy, affection, love. To the extent that we allow ourselves to fully experience our whole range of feelings, we move toward health-fullness.

It is tempting to manipulate our experiences to meet our desires or expectations, screening out "bad" feelings and acknowledging only "good" ones, or vice versa—tempting, but dangerous. While extreme ups and downs may be disruptive to life, or even signal underlying problems that need to be resolved, the pursuit of emotional stability at any cost is probably even less healthy. People who are always moderate, never ruffled, and always evenkeeled are probably shutting out or at least toning down some feelings. Unfortunately, feelings are rather rebellious devils, and when we deny them they often go underground only to burst out at some later—usually inappropriate—time and place.

We're not advocating temper tantrums or promiscuity. Angry feelings can be experienced without being expressed directly or destructively. Sexual attraction can be enjoyed without being indulged. We are advocating awareness, paying attention to the signals our psyche sends us, and exercise, allowing ourselves to experience the depth and breadth of our emotional capacity.

We need not be at the mercy of our bodily sensations and psychic impulses. Feelings are controlled by our mind, not by external events. We create our feelings and reactions based on the way we interpret what's going on around us. If we view a situation as a *threat,* feelings of hurt, fear, anger, and pain will follow. If we view it as a *treat,* feelings of comfort, joy, belonging, and anticipation result. If we really want to feel differently, all we need is a new set of glasses for viewing the world.

A note of caution: a blowup of negative feelings may simply be your warning system signaling that something in your life is not right. If you experience sudden, sharp abdominal pain, you probably will want to check out the source of the problem. The same applies to emotional pain. Rather than deny the feelings, pay attention to their implicit request that you take a look at your life and see what's gone haywire.

*How about you? How wide is your emotional spec-*

*trum? What feelings do you tend to screen out? Which are your most frequent companions?*

## THREE TIPS FOR FEELING "GOOD"

**Stretch your feeling capacity.** Feelings are at the heart of life. Yet most of us lack the vocabulary to distinguish and describe the subtle nuances of our experiences. Shades of love include affection, tenderness, admiration, liking, attraction, caring. We may hate, despise, dislike, or feel indifferent. Attraction may take the form of desire, longing, craving, coveting, or hankering. Hope leads us to anticipate, trust, rely, feel confident. Despair may take the form of desperation, despondency, doubt, suspicion, discouragement, disappointment, defeat, helplessness. Next time you feel frightened, try to pinpoint the exact color and intensity of your emotion. Are you paralyzed? Apprehensive? Anxious? Panicky? Scared stiff? Terrified? Aroused? Exhilarated? Worried? Troubled? Disquieted? Uneasy? Appalled? Timid? Alarmed? Petrified? Jumpy? As you expand your feeling-word vocabulary, you may be surprised to discover a new depth and richness in your experiences.

**Look for the silver linings.** Choose to be positive. Every coin has two sides. Every experience both a cost and a benefit; every life, an up side and a down side. Choose a positive mental attitude. Trust in yourself. Trust in your life. Saying "everything will work out OK in the end" is phony only if you do nothing to help it work out. Laugh rather than complain. Play "ain't it funny" rather than "ain't it awful." Pop mental bubbles with humor.

**Practice the attitude of gratitude.** To a great extent our attitude determines the kinds of feelings we experience. A cynical, fearful, negative attitude will fill us with negative experience. A positive, hopeful, open attitude will fill us with warmth. Hans Selye, renowned stress researcher, claims that hate and revenge are harmful to our physical health, while optimal physical functioning is associated with the attitude of gratitude. Poisoning your life by attempting to get even hurts only you. "I'll get you, if it's the last thing I do" may very well be the last thing you do! Obsession with hate and revenge erodes our bodies, our minds, and our spirits—not to mention our relationships with others. Love and thankfulness will open your life and fill it with vitality and healing.

## DEVELOPING YOUR SENSE OF SELF

One of the best ways to stay mentally health-full is to know, respect, and like yourself. In short, to maintain a healthy self-concept.

For some of us that's no easy task. We bombard ourselves with a nonstop commentary on our thoughts, feelings, behavior, appearance: "You klutz!" "Simmer down now," "Next to her you look like a tank," "Stupid!" "You never finish anything," "You'd better not!" "She doesn't like me," "He thinks I'm empty-headed," "That's crazy," "If you were a stronger person you could stop," "You creep," "You're never going to make it." It's tough to keep a sense of perspective in the face of all those critical messages. Fortunately this irrational self-talk is often contradicted by feedback from others and from the environment—and occasionally even from within ourselves. Our worst fears are not confirmed. You move gracefully through the room. He praises your memo. She invites you to play racquetball. Your "crazy" idea inspires a new ad campaign. You *do* make it. Somehow we survive these mental gymnastics, some of us with more self-esteem than others.

We all have our own levels of intelligence, our own strengths and limitations, our own emotional patterns and personal characteristics that contribute to our own sense of self. When we can authentically affirm all these dimensions of self, including our inadequacies, we are better able to meet life's challenges. With a positive self-concept we can face up to the problems we encounter, feeling confident and optimistic about our capacity to cope effectively with them.

*How about you? In what ways does your sense of self enhance your health-fullness? What are some of your favorite personal putdowns? What qualities of yours do you particularly admire?*

Here are a few strategies for promoting your self-esteem that have been particularly helpful to us in our personal lives and our work with clients.

## SIX SELF-ESTEEM BUILDERS

**Talk to yourself gently.** Are you your own worst critic? What do you say to yourself as you go through your day? Call yourself bad names and you'll end up a lot more fatigued than if you whisper sweet somethings. Remember the last time you were embarrassed? Did you say to yourself, "Oh, you dummy, look what a fool you are!"? Why not change that self-talk to, "Look at all the attention I'm getting," or "It's OK, I learn from my mistakes." Instead of saying, "I want everyone to like me," why not say, "Ninety-nine percent is good enough." Instead of, "I should get everything I want when I want it!" why not say, "I'll never get all that I want." Do you get the point? Try to counter your irrational self-talk with positive messages that let you off the hook.

**Be realistic.** Accept your limits as part of your humanness, not as blemishes to be eradicated. So you have a high-pitched voice. So your mind is boggled by numbers. So your foot turns out. So your hair is coarse. So you don't like everyone you meet. So you can't act on all your ideas. So what! If no one else notices your good points, pat yourself on the back. Sprinkle your shortcomings with a grain of salt. Avoid comparisons—especially with an "ideal you" based on everyone else's best traits.

**Worry wisely.** Avoid worrying prematurely about what might happen in the future. When Angie and John anxiously pressed their doctor about how long their diabetic son might live, he wisely replied, "If you cross the bridge before you get there, you'll have to pay the toll twice." When you can't control the outcome, let go. Mark Twain once said, "I've seen a great many problems in life and most of them never happened." Surrender! Some things you simply can't change. You aren't God. Don't hit your head against a stone wall. When you can influence the outcome, worry only long enough to warm up for action. Try to live without regrets. Surrender to the flow of life. Let go and laugh.

**Affirm your resources.** Attend to your internal sources of strength. Keep them in mind and make them work for you, whatever they are. Mother Teresa was asked, "What are the sources of your strength?" She replied, "A 98-year-old woman in Philadelphia who prays for me." Strength is around you and within you. If you get centered and bring your strength alive in your mind, it will work for you. Spend some time alone with yourself, centering in to your internal resources.

**Focus on what deeply satisfies you.** Occupy yourself and your time with projects, commitments, challenges, and people that help you feel worthwhile. Don't just put in time laboring at repetitive or meaningless work. Even if you have to "labor" to keep a roof over your head, spend as much energy as possible in your "lifework." Invest yourself in some creative, meaningful activity that gives you a sense of purpose and worth. You may volunteer respite care for parents of a handicapped child or telephone for United Way or work your 40 hours in critical care. For mental health it's important that you're able to say, "I'm useful," "I held up my end," "I did good!"

**Hang in there when the going gets tough.** When you feel as if your world is falling apart and you think you're going to pieces, don't withdraw from your meaningful commitments. If you do, you'll feel useless and confirm your sense of falling to pieces. Try to keep performing your responsibilities as normally as possible. Tell yourself, "I'm strong enough," "I can manage," "I will grow from this experience."

## REFLECTIONS

Before we move to consider relational self-care, please stop and reflect on your overall mental-self-care habits. Do they enhance or erode your health-fullness?

---

### Personal Reflection on My Mental Health

My intellectual patterns (curiosity, learning, creativity, openness to challenges, control of energy investment)

---

---

My emotional patterns (acceptance and range of feelings, positive outlook, gratitude, revenge)

---

---

My self-esteem patterns (internal dialogs, worry, strengths, meaningful work, affirmation)

_____

_____

## Wish List for Mental Health-Fullness

List here everything you can imagine wanting for your mental health-fullness. What would you like to be able to do? To know? To feel? To learn? Let your imagination run free. Don't limit yourself in any way. The wishes don't have to be practical. Have fun dreaming.

I wish I could:

_____

_____

_____

_____

## THOUGHT PROVOKERS

### For Individual Reflection and Group Discussion

1. As a group, make a list of all the feeling words you can think of. Be sure to get over 100, representing a broad spectrum of emotions.

Come to a consensus of your group's top five favorite emotions and your group's five least favorite feelings. Take care that all opinions receive serious consideration in reaching your consensus.

Which emotions on your list do you think Jesus felt? Are there any you think that he never felt? Share your opinions on the issue, then read one of the Gospels and note all the verses that portray Jesus' emotions in word or action.

2. Recall a recent experience where something in your life really went wrong. What were the circumstances? What was supposed to happen? What did happen? Why? What got messed up?

Tell the story of the incident to someone else by setting the situation carefully. Then describe in great detail what happened. Dramatize the scene, exaggerate the feelings and incongruities.

The humor of your dilemma may emerge when you describe the irony of what happened rather than complain about your disappointment.

3. Think of someone you're holding a grudge against. Remember the person and the incident that led to your broken relationship. Right now force yourself to write a letter of gratitude toward that person. Don't be cynical or sarcastic. Express your true appreciation. Be thankful for something and see how it changes your attitude. If you're in a group, read the letter aloud and talk about your feelings.

Remember, revenge eats you alive—not the other person, but you! Gratitude fills you—not the other person, but you!

4. Fill in the blanks in the following sentences:
I believe I am _____ and I am _____ and I am _____ .
But I also am _____ and _____ .
Sometimes I am _____ and often _____ . Seldom am I _____ and I'm never _____ . But when you get right down to it, I am always _____ .
Read your answers aloud in the group and then expand your list. What do you notice about your self-image?

# 5

# Fill Me with Love
## Relational Self-Care

In the early 1960s Sidney Jourard hypothesized that people who loved deeply would live longer. This pioneer in the field of intentional relationship-building believed that if we revealed ourselves to one another we would live vital, high-energy lives with less sickness and suffering.

Jourard's theory has recently been substantiated by the results of a longitudinal study of "healthy" men. These 200 men were followed for 40 years after graduation from college to determine what factors would distinguish the healthy group from those who were disabled or deceased. Surprisingly, the crucial difference was not salt intake or exercise or weight control. The key to health was self-disclosure. The healthy group reported the consistent presence in their lives of at least one individual with whom they could share their thoughts and feelings. For some men this sympathetic ear belonged to a spouse; for others it was a friend or colleague.

## ISOLATION IS SICKENING

This study reinforces what common sense and folk wisdom has known for centuries: loneliness and alienation make people sick. In Old Testament times a person excluded from community was considered to be dead. In a similar way people sicken and die outside of human community.

Choosing to develop rich and meaningful relationships is a vital survival skill. A supportive network of friends who offer understanding, closeness, and fellowship enhances your potential for health-fullness.

How about you? How many people know you deeply and understand who you really are? We hope that you can name at least one—three or four would be even better.


## DEVELOPING HEALTHY RELATIONSHIPS

Healthy relationships are characterized by reciprocal responsibilities and mutual satisfaction. When both people are committed to give and take, to sharing and listening, both partners' needs are satisfied in the exchange. Since this chapter focuses on self-care, we're going to look at the receiving side of relationships here and save the giving dimension for the next part on reaching out.

If you find it difficult to focus on your own needs rather than on others, remember the results of the study. The healthy men actively sought out relationships that would meet their needs. So can you. And you can reap the same reward—health.

*Think back over the past week. How fulfilling were your interactions with others? Did you feel alone even when you were with others? Did you feel rejected? Ignored? Let down? Did you get the impression that people misunderstood or didn't appreciate you? Did you feel isolated, going it alone without support? Did you feel forgotten or left out, uninvolved? Did you feel pressured, overburdened with responsibility to others? Did you feel drained, as if you'd given your very last ounce of caring?*

Everyone experiences these feelings once in a while. However, if the feelings are familiar and frequent for you, it may be a sign that you need to work on improving your support network. The suggestions on the following pages may help you nurture the health of your relationships.

## PRACTICE SELF-DISCLOSURE

Sharing yourself with others is a matter of choice, not chance. Some people choose openness; others tend to hide their inner selves. Each of us faces the decision hundreds of times each day: "Shall I say what's really in my heart and share myself as I really am inside, or not?" "Should I maintain my public self, or let my private self sneak out?"

People who keep up a good front, never talking about their problems and deepest fears, cut themselves off from a major source of healing and support. What you won't share with anyone else is usually something you need to hear, something you are unwilling to accept about you. When you succeed in putting up a good front, you lose touch with yourself and your heart.

Excuses for not sharing are endless: "He won't be interested," "They won't understand," "Don't wash your dirty linen in public," "I'm not that close to anyone," "My life is just too hectic, there's no time," "She's got more troubles than I have." All are potentially accurate statements, but not good excuses for closing yourself off.

Obviously, it's inappropriate to "spill your guts" indiscriminately. Sometimes it's better to keep your mouth shut. But most of the time with some special people, or some of the time with most people, you need to share yourself for *your* benefit, for *your* health. It's just too exhausting to maintain your public self all the time. We all need someone—at least one someone—who knows and accepts our private self too.

*How about you? To what degree is your public self different from your private self? How much of yourself are you willing to share with your spouse? Your children? Your parents? Your best friend? Your work associates? People in general? What would you be unwilling to share with these particular people?*

*What kinds of things have you never shared with anyone? Your innermost fears? A painful experience? Something of which you aren't proud? Your greatest joys or accomplishments? Pick something you've not shared. Determine to disclose that experience with someone during the next week. Who will it be? When will you do it?*

*A note of warning:* if you know what you want to share would be hurtful to the other person, find someone else to listen to this particular feeling or experience. It's tempting to use sharing as retaliation. That's not the point here.

## KNOW YOUR NEEDS

Each of us has a variety of interpersonal needs. In order to feel connected with others we must be plugged into a support network that satisfies these needs. Interpersonal support may come from many sources and take many forms, but all of us require that our basic needs be met on a regular basis.

Sometimes we just need the support of someone who will *listen* intently to whatever is on our mind or heart. Paul Tournier, Swiss theologian and physician, reflected, "It is impossible to overemphasize the immense need people have to be really listened to, to be taken seriously, to be understood."

At other times we need *emotional nurture,* the unconditional positive regard that lets us know beyond the shadow of a doubt that we are loved and cherished —just as we are, without one plea.

Support may also take the form of *feedback*—honest information that gives us an opportunity to check our perception of reality with someone else's viewpoint. This kind of mirror holding is a rare gift when we ask for it and respect the giver. It's a little less easy to take when it's unsolicited.

Whether our lifework is parenting or painting or providing services to others, each of us needs interpersonal support to sustain and enrich our on-the-job efforts. On occasion we need *commendation*—positive feedback about our skills and accomplishments. We need to be praised for a job well done and appreciated for our unique contributions.

As in the personal arena, we all need *challenge* as well—feedback and information that stimulates us to stretch and grow. Although it's tough to listen to criticism without defensiveness, we all need such opportunities to learn about ourselves.

Finally, all of us need someone with whom we can share laughter and *play* time, satisfying our abiding need for re-creation.

Who fills these interpersonal needs for you? One person? Several people? Different people at different times? Think of all the people you know and interact with: friends, work associates, close family, relatives, church acquaintances, neighbors, clients, store clerks, service people, club members. All of these relationships serve a purpose, meet some need for you. They can potentially be a source of interpersonal support and vitalization, or a source of disappointment.

## STOP AND REFLECT

To whom do you look primarily in your life right now to fulfill your interpersonal needs?

| | To whom do you look? | How successfully are your needs met? | Who else could possibly fill this need? |
|---|---|---|---|
| Listening | | | |
| Emotional Nurture | | | |
| Feedback | | | |
| Commendation | | | |
| Challenge | | | |
| Play | | | |

As you review your relationships from this perspective, you may want to keep these ideas in mind.

# FIVE PRINCIPLES FOR GETTING
## YOUR NEEDS MET

**Don't put all your eggs in one basket.** It is extremely unlikely that one person can meet all of your interpersonal needs. Don't depend on a single soul to function as your entire support network.

**Don't beat your head against a stone wall.** Frustration results when we expect an inappropriate person to meet a particular need. Don't bother looking for listening from someone you know can't or won't come through. Don't expect your workaholic roommate to take time out for jumping in a leaf pile.

**Accept willing substitutes.** Even if there's a vacant position (spouse, best friend, father confessor) in your life for a time, you can still find people to meet each of your interpersonal needs.

**Don't wait for a mind reader.** Intentionality is essential in human relationships. Know what you need and search out someone to help you satisfy that need. You have to reveal yourself to get your needs met. Ask for what you want. It's foolish to say to yourself, "If they really loved me they would *know* what I want without my asking." It's foolish to make other people guess what you need. When you do, you're less likely to receive what would fill you.

**Speak up.** It's risky to ask for what you want. Others might not give it to you. Or if they do, you may discover that it's not as satisfying as you had imagined. However, the risks of rejection and dissatisfaction seem small in comparison to the risks of isolation, loneliness, and frustration.

When you find yourself feeling isolated and lonely, it's likely that you're not getting all of what you need from others. It might be necessary for you to carefully analyze the support you're missing and intentionally pull together a support network to help you fill the gaps in your relationship.

## KNOW AND NURTURE YOUR
## SUPPORT NETWORK

The average person knows well over 10,000 people in a lifetime—family, work colleagues, church members, neighbors, boyfriends, sales clerks, former teachers, fellow students, public figures, auto mechanics, friends, friends of friends. Our contacts increase in ever-wider ripples, expanding our potential support network.

Most people don't intentionally convert that *potential* into an *actual* support system. Unless you clearly identify your support network, you probably won't take steps to nurture it and help it grow. You are surrounded by hundreds of pairs of smiling eyes waiting to be drafted into your army of supporters. Who are they?

Identify your support network by drawing a circle on a sheet of paper. Put your name in the circle. Then think first about the persons with whom you have the strongest bonds and identify them by name around you. Then add people with whom you have less frequent or more casual contact. Continue diagramming and adding names as long as you can. Then use your address book or photograph album to jog your memory some more. List as many people as you like.

Think about each person in the diagram and remember the warmth and closeness you've shared. Pick one or two people you'd especially like to have positive contact with right now. Plan to make that contact via phone or in person during the next 24 hours.

# START A SUPPORT GROUP

A support group is a gathering of people who make a commitment to meet regularly and listen, share, and care. A bowling team may be supportive, but it's not a support group. A coffee circle may be supportive, but it's not a support group either. A support group is an intentional gathering for the direct purpose of giving and receiving support.

A true support group involves equal exchange among peers. There is no designated leader and no status hierarchy. When choosing support group members, pick people you think would be helpful to you. They don't have to be your best friends. Some people you hardly know could be excellent sources of interpersonal support. Remember—this group is for *you*. Don't select people who you think would benefit from a group unless they also can meet some of your needs.

The basis of the group—the glue, if you will—is commitment over time. Plan to meet together at least twice a month for six months. Make support group a top priority.

Be ready to share yourself. In sharing yourself you learn to know yourself more fully.

Be ready to support and be supported. Support starts with your presence and care-full listening.

Give yourselves time to become a group. Don't hurry. Take time to tell your stories, to get acquainted in depth.

Make a clear contract with each other regarding listening to feelings, sharing of feelings, problem solving, off-limit areas, and confidentiality.

Give no feedback unless it's asked for. A support group is not an encounter group, and it's not therapy, although it may be therapeutic. Unsolicited feedback is inappropriate. Keep it to yourself.

Know that the needs of the people in the group will change. Set periodic times to reevaluate individual needs and redefine your contract with one another.

_____

If you were to start a support group, whom would *you like* to invite?

_____    _____

_____    _____

_____

Don't be afraid to risk. Some people you ask will be interested and others won't. Gather those who are interested. If you still need more people, come up with additional names together. Then gather the group, make your commitment to one another, and see what happens over the months.

## WATCH OUT FOR PEOPLE TRAPS

Although relationships can be wonderful health enhancers, it's easy to get caught in unhealthy relationship patterns that sap your energy and leave you unfulfilled and fatigued. Beware of these three typical tangles.

**Pleasing others.** If you try to please everyone and make sure everyone always approves of you 100 percent, you're 100 percent guaranteed to end up exhausted and disappointed. Trying to please everyone is an impossible goal, a no-win endeavor!

**Taking on too much responsibility.** If you seldom say no, requests from others may soon overwhelm you. This is just another form of trying to please everyone. To stay healthy you'll have to learn to limit yourself to caring only for those most important to you.

This trap catches many of us in the middle years

when we're surrounded by demands from growing children *and* from aging parents, both generations struggling with dependence and independence. When you're in that spot, it's understandable that you sometimes feel exhausted and discouraged. Try not to add anyone else to your caring list at that point; your hands are full. In a few more years you'll be ready to volunteer for relationship duty again. For the present time, find some ways to get your own needs met.

**Playing the game of "Poor Lonely Me."** Loneliness is being alone when you don't want to be. It hurts, but it's not the end of the world, and it doesn't have to be permanent.

Withdrawing into your shell and feeling sorry for yourself will only perpetuate the problem and won't get you much sympathy anyway. So, take action on your own behalf.

First, accept the fact that you're lonely, and let the feelings be. Don't try to change them with eating, drinking, surface relationships, or irresponsible sex. Just accept yourself as you are right now.

Second, find someone you can talk to about your feelings. Confide in someone—even if you have to pay a therapist to listen.

Third, experiment with changes in your patterns of living that will help break down your isolation. If you haven't found a way to meet another best friend, then try volunteering with the elderly or reading books to the blind. Don't sit at home like a shut-in waiting for someone to come to you. Reach out in some way to break out of your loneliness.

## REFLECTION

Before we move on to consider spiritual self-care, please stop and think through your patterns of relating to others. Do your current relationships and your relationship habits enhance or erode your level of healthfullness?

_____

## Personal Reflection on My Relationships

My self-disclosure patterns:

_____
_____

My basic need fulfillment:

_____
_____

My support network:

_____
_____

My negative habits (traps):

_____
_____

## Wish List for My Social Health

Write down here everything you can imagine wanting for your relational health. What would you feel like? Who would you relate to? Who would you like to meet? Let your imagination run free. Don't limit yourself in any way. The wishes do not have to be practical. Have fun dreaming.

I wish I could:

_____
_____
_____
_____

## THOUGHT PROVOKERS

### For Individual Reflection and Group Discussion

1. Play the game "Poor Lonely Me." The rules of the game are simple. Describe to your group your

loneliness, your misery, how much you give to others, how overburdened you are, how alone you are, how you're forgotten, how no one understands or appreciates you—as dramatically as possible.

Do try to top the stories of others. Show clearly how you are much worse off than they are. Convince your group that you are the "poorest, loneliest me" there ever was. (Try to take this seriously. Don't laugh. After all, most of us practice this game regularly; we just don't make it so obvious!)

You may want the psalmist to start first. Here's what he said:

Save me O God!
The water is up to my neck;
I am sinking in deep mud,
    and there is no solid ground;
I am out in deep water,
    and the waves are about to drown me.
I am worn out from calling for help,
    and my throat is aching    (Ps. 69:1-3 TEV).

Top his story!

After you've finished storytelling, talk about how you felt doing this exercise, and how you feel now.

2. At the top of one side of a blank piece of paper put MY PUBLIC SELF. Then list all the experiences, history, and feeling characteristics about you that you're generally comfortable talking about and sharing with others.

At the top of the other side of the paper put MY PRIVATE SELF and list all the experiences, history, and feeling characteristics about you that you are not comfortable sharing with others.

Compare the size of the two lists. What do you observe? If you shared some of your private side, what do you imagine would happen?

Select one item from your private-self side and share it with your group. What happened? How do you feel? Did your fantasy come true?

3. Complete the worksheet on interpersonal needs in this chapter. Then share your observations and insights with your group or with a friend or family member.

4. *The Mind-Reading Dilemma* shows you how foolish it is to hope that others will read your mind and give you what you want without your even asking. It will also help you practice asking for what you want.

On an index card write down something you want right now from someone in your group or from your whole group ("Get off my back," "Please notice me," "Invite me to play racquetball"). Be specific—specific wants, specific person.

One by one, everyone in the group should try to guess what you wrote on the card. See how close they do or don't come to predicting what you wanted. After all have had a turn to guess, then read what's on your card. Next, look at the person(s) named on your want card and say "Will you give me this?"

Then listen for the answers to your request. The other(s) may say yes or no. That's the risk you each take. You may not get what you wanted, but at least you asked clearly.

How do you feel? What did you learn by asking for what you want rather than waiting for someone to read your mind?

5. In Taylor Caldwell's novel *The Listener*, people in pain and despair, people burdened with every type of problem, enter the Listener's room and come out healed. At the end of the story the reader finally enters

the room to meet the Listener—and finds only a crucifix.

Jesus is a good listener, and he has promised to bear our burdens and heal our iniquities. What would you want to tell him were you to enter that room?

- Write a dialog of your healing encounter with the Listener.
- Read your dialog out loud.
- Then burn your notes in a fireplace or ashtray. Watch them burn. Give your story up to God— and know that you are accepted, forgiven, and no longer alone.

# 6

# **Magic Moments**
## Spiritual Self-Care

When we were youngsters, the Hollywood fad was 3-D movies. With your ticket you received a pair of cardboard glasses with one green lens, one red. The remarkable contraptions brought a third dimension to movie viewing—depth.

Spiritual reality is the depth dimension of life. In order to focus on this aspect of health-fullness, you'll need your own set of 3-D glasses, with its matching vocabulary. Our Christian spectacles give us a particular viewpoint and words to bring our spiritual beliefs into focus. We describe our experience and endow it with meaning in a way that seems comfortable and proper to us. Your perspective and language will do the same for you.

We don't want to say that one set of glasses or another is the correct one for all. Rather, we encourage you to get out your spectacles, whatever they are, and polish them up so that you can view spiritual health at its maximum depth, color, and impact. We'll use examples from our experience. Feel free to translate as necessary into whatever language and images are meaning-full to you.

## THE SPIRIT CONNECTION

Health and wholeness are essentially spiritual concepts. In general, Americans don't spend much time focusing on the spiritual dimension of life. Consequently we don't know as much about health and wholeness as we'd like. The time has come for us to accept the spiritual as an important—perhaps the most important—dimension of well-being.

Most of us know intuitively that medical treatments, or any of the self-care remedies we've examined so far, are not powerful enough to heal us if the spirit is fractured. We all know people whose physical health has failed because they've lost purpose in life. We know others whose guilt feelings are so profound that mental health or satisfying relationships seem like unattainable goals.

The power of the spirit manifests itself even more dramatically in the many inspiring accounts of people whose faith has made them whole. Our friend Jean miraculously survived life-threatening illness and surgery. None of the physicians expected her to live. The anesthesiologist came to visit her three times before she left the hospital. Each time he said things like, "Some things you just can't explain" and "You have an extraordinary will to live." It seemed obvious that his medical knowledge couldn't explain to him why she had not died. The activity of the spirit and the will, along with hope, can be catalysts that mobilize our healing resources in ways that our reason cannot understand.

The Swiss psychiatrist Carl Jung was convinced that

spiritual concerns are the central components of health, observing: "Among my patients in the second half of life there has not been one whose problem in the last resort was not that of finding a religious outlook on life . . . and none of them really has been healed who did not regain his religious outlook."

Jesus' ministry was filled with incidents that clearly connected health with the human spirit. The blind were given their sight, the lame could walk again, the troubled were purged of "demons," social outcasts were welcomed into fellowship. All were healed on the strength of their belief and their contrite hearts—their spiritual health.

Your values, beliefs, and commitments can be the key to your health as well. The spiritual dimension of life can be either a source of distress or a powerful resource for health. Let's take a closer look at the phenomenon of spiritual health.

## WHAT IS SPIRITUAL HEALTH?

Although religious beliefs and practices may contribute to spiritual health, spiritual health is by no means determined only by the rituals and dogma of the organized church. When we use the word *spiritual* here, we are referring to that core dimension of you—your innermost self—where you have a profound sense of who you are, where you came from, where you're going, and how you might reach that point.

In addition to supplying meaning for life, the spiritual dimension provides you with principles for living and explains to you why the universe works the way it does. Commitment to God or some ultimate concern engenders a spirit of selflessness, sensitivity to others, and a willingness to sacrifice for people in need. The spiritual dimension of life recognizes a power beyond the natural and rational, accepts on faith the unknown or difficult to explain, and provides a framework for understanding death. Rituals and ceremonies create structures for attending to and expressing our spiritual selves.

*How about you? To what extent are you attuned to your spiritual core? Do you consider yourself a deep person? A spirit-filled person? A religious person? What part does God play in your life? Would you say you are spiritually healthy?*

Compare the qualities of spiritual health and spiritual atrophy we've gathered below. Which collection more accurately describes your current condition?

| Spiritual Health | Spiritual Atrophy |
|---|---|
| hope | emptiness |
| positive outlook | anxiety |
| acceptance of death | loss of meaning |
| forgiveness, self-acceptance | long dry spells |
| commitment | apathy |
| meaning and purpose | dead at the core |
| clear values | looking for "magic" |
| sense of worth | conflicting values |
| peace | needing to prove myself |
| in touch with God | hurried and harried |
| worship, prayer, meditation | self-absorption |

No matter what your present position on the atrophy–health continuum, there are positive steps you can take to enhance your spiritual health and consequently your overall well-being.

## GET IN TOUCH WITH YOUR CORE

*Who are you? Where did you come from? Where are you going? When all the surface layers are peeled away, what do you believe is at the core of life? What is at the core of you?*

The process of touching and being touched by your core is an experience that creates wholeness and gives you energy. When people are out of touch with what's central in life—focusing on the periphery—they become dis-spirited and de-energized.

Enthusiasm, that bubbling of life energy, comes from tapping into the spirit of God within—deep within. The Greek root word for *enthusiasm* originally means "in God"—in touch with the energy of the divine, filled with and able to express God's energy as it flows through. When you're in touch with that energy, you know you're alive. Today we use *enthusiasm* to mean fervent, passionate, positive mental interest and have almost forgotten the divine spirit meaning —but it's still there.

At times people are receptive to spiritual reflection, at other times they are not. At times spiritual realities barge in on our lives and we are ready to deal with them. At other times we are not ready and don't sense the need at all.

How do you go about getting in touch with your core? For starters, you can set up an atmosphere that invites spiritual reflection, that helps get you ready. The five postures for spiritual growth suggest some strategies for tuning in to your spiritual core.

**Be quiet.** Spiritual truths often come in the form of a still small voice that is difficult to hear above the chaos and confusion of a frantic life-style. Set aside time for solitude and meditation.

**Be open to the spiritual.** Spiritual experiences often come in unexpected forms and packages. They surprise us. Foster a nonjudgmental attitude so that you're open to the spiritual dimension in any life event—from hoeing the garden to witnessing an accident, from watching a swim meet to reading the morning paper. God may be waiting in the wings to touch your core.

**Be inquisitive and curious.** An attitude of active searching increases your options and potential for spiritual centering. Don't shut doors before you check out what's behind them. For example, laying on of hands may be a powerful centering experience. Through interpersonal Bible study you may discover whole new dimensions of yourself. A silent retreat might renew your enthusiasm.

**Be receptive to pain and grief.** Pain helps us focus on the widest questions of our being. It's a deepener. A life without pain leads to a sparse, shallow existence. Feel your pain fully, then ask, "What is it trying to teach me?"

**Be playful.** Play is a pleasurable, freeing experience. It breeds spontaneous enthusiasm and celebration. When you make music, dance, laugh, sing—however you play—listen for sounds of the spirit.


## TRY SEEING WITH YOUR SOUL

Spiritual experiences take many forms. Can you recall times when you felt depth and centeredness? When you were touched by an eternal truth, and you knew you were on holy ground? An evening worship experience? A moment of great sorrow at death? A sunset? A storm? A word of forgiveness and love? A period of intense pain? A sense of unity with everything living? Sometimes these touching moments are high "mountaintop" experiences, sometimes they are deep reflective experiences. But whether we sink deep into ourselves or soar out beyond our usual boundaries of the self, at these moments we are in touch with the eternal and have tapped into a source of energy much greater than ourselves.

Most spiritual experiences transcend the images of physical time and space that we typically call reality.

At these moments we see beyond the limits. We see with our soul, not with our eyes. We know, not with the mind, but with the heart. This special knowing and seeing is a rare gift. Periodically we need to give ourselves space and quiet—to sit down by the side of the road and let our souls catch up to us.

## REDISCOVERING THE DEPTH DIMENSION

Oil is discovered not by drilling 1000 one-foot holes, but by drilling one 1000-foot hole. We grow in spiritual vision by contemplating the meaning of the deepest, most touching moments of our lives—and by letting these experiences guide our vision and our decisions.

*Recall a few of the most "touching" moments in your life. What deep truth did you discover or rediscover in each of these "soul times"? How did these experiences energize you? Describe the wisdom and perspective you gained in these special times of depth. How has this new view educated and guided your decisions?*

How can you stay in touch with these truths and regularly promote your spiritual health? Most religious traditions suggest that the process of being in relationship with the Creator has health-giving potential. When we set aside time for reflection, meditation, and prayer, we provide opportunity for staying in touch with and being touched by the source of life and health. St. Paul encourages Christians to meditate as follows:

> Fill your minds with those things that are good and that deserve praise: things that are true, noble, right, pure, lovely, and honorable. Put into practice what you have learned and received from me, both from my words and from my actions. And the God who gives us peace will be with you (Phil. 4:8-9 TEV).

*What about you? Do you provide space in your day for spiritual reflection? How satisfied are you with the level and quality of that commitment? In what ways could you increase your spiritual depth?*

## EXPAND YOUR IMAGES OF HEALTH

As you expand your awareness of the spiritual dimension of health, you will discover more and more qualities that contribute to your wholeness and well-being. We've collected a dozen virtues that could potentially fill your life and enhance your health. As you read them, consider each image carefully. Meditate on them one by one. Get a sense of the positive difference they make for you as you focus your attention and allow them to fill you.

### Twelve Elements of Spiritual Health

LOVE: the commitment to be present, to invest in another rather than remain self-engrossed. To whom have you committed yourself in love?

INTIMACY: the choice to abandon isolation and independence in favor of heartfelt sharing, mutual support, and interdependence. With whom are you intimate?

TRUST: the willingness to be vulnerable instead of cautious, suspicious, and cynical. In what ways do you allow yourself to be vulnerable? With whom?

MEANING: a clear sense of direction, no longer drifting without purpose at the mercy of life's winds and waves. What gives you a sense of direction? Where are you headed?

HOPE: the vision of a desirable future, a present pregnant with promise, eager to be born with our help. What is your vision of your future?

FAITH: the unquestioning leap of faith, relinquishing fear and uncertainty to affirm the not yet proven. What are your convictions?

COMMITMENT: the decision to invest rather than straddle the fence, to move toward a goal with energy and endurance. Where have you invested yourself with strength and perseverance?

PATIENCE: the willingness to wait, allowing the future its chance to emerge, no longer pushing the river to make life happen. How and when do you wait expectantly and patiently?

JOY: the rush of delight that fills an empty shell. When do you let yourself bubble with joy?

IMAGINATION: the new view, the creative spark that challenges habit and boredom. What would be some new options for you?

COURAGE: the willingness to face limitations and still risk rather than playing it safe or being defensive. When have you ventured in spite of your limits?

GRATITUDE: the thankful appreciation that counteracts the myth of self-sufficiency. For what are you truly thankful?

After considering this evidence of depth in your life, how would you judge your spiritual health?

## FOUR CAUTIONS

Cynicism closes down the spirit as effectively as a lethal herbicide. Although our spiritual nature is deep, its flowers are often fragile. When you feel a spell of cynicism coming on, look for something to cherish or celebrate instead.

Religion or church activities may actually get in the way of spiritual experience if we let them obscure the underlying meaning. Be careful when dogma becomes more important than depth, the trivial more important than the touch. Rigid, narrow, judgmental thinking can close off opportunities for your spirit to stretch and grow.

It's tempting to ignore the spirit dimension of life since the consequences of spiritlessness usually don't show up until crisis points. Spirits suffer from inattention and neglect without complaint. They rust silently from lack of use. Don't count on your core for help in crises unless you've nourished and exercised it regularly.

## REFLECTION

Please stop and consider again your overall patterns of spiritual self-care. Do your spiritual habits enhance or erode your level of health-fullness? What is your personal spiritual philosophy?

---

### Personal Reflection on My Spiritual Health

What values, beliefs, and commitments do I most cherish?

---

---

How do these central spiritual truths enhance my health?

---

---

Which aspects of spirit are missing or weak in my life?

---

---

What rituals do I find meaningful and helpful for promoting my spiritual depth?

_____

_____

How could I increase their healing effects?

_____

_____

What advice could I give younger persons that might
help them develop a richer spiritual life?

_____

_____

### Wish List for My Spiritual Health

Write down here everything you can imagine wanting
for yourself spiritually. How would you like to feel?
Act? What would you like to be? Let your imagination
run free. Don't limit yourself in any way. The wishes do
not have to be "practical." Have fun dreaming.

I wish I could:

_____

_____

_____

_____

## THOUGHT PROVOKERS

### For Individual Reflection and Group Discussion

1. Review the five postures for spiritual growth discussed in this chapter. Then answer these questions
thoughtfully in writing.

**Be quiet.**

How has the noise of a hectic life-style gotten in
your way lately?

What specific noises have made it difficult for you
to hear the small voice within you?

What do you think this voice is whispering that you've been missing?

**Be open to the spiritual.**

When have you shut out unexpected or unusual spiritual experiences?

What kinds of surprises have you missed?

What preconceived notions close you off?

**Be inquisitive and curious.**

If you were to actually search for new forms of spiritual experience, what kinds might be revealing, even though they may not be like your normal style? (Prayer groups? Silence? Alternative worship styles?)

What do you think you might learn if you experimented with one of these?

What specifically would you be afraid of?

**Be receptive to pain and grief.**

What pain have you tried to block out or ignore?

If you listen to it, what do you think it will teach you about your depth?

What are you afraid of?

**Be playful.**

When have you been so serious that you missed a chance to celebrate and grow in the spirit?

Where did you learn that you should be so serious in spiritual matters?

Why do you keep believing this?

What do you think you could learn by lightening up a bit and becoming more playful?

2. What vocabulary are you most comfortable using when discussing spiritual self-care? What spiritual vocabulary makes you uncomfortable?

Discuss this issue with your group. Try—for five minutes—to talk about your spiritual experiences using a language different from your normal style. How do you feel? What do you learn?

Find someone whose spiritual vocabulary and understanding is quite different from yours. Discuss the issue of spiritual health with this person, listening closely and trying to understand his or her experience fully.

3. List the "miracle" experiences in your own life, the times when whatever occurred had little rational explanation and seemed to be due to a power beyond you.

Remember and refeel their depth. Experience the clarity and enthusiasm again. Thank God for them.

Describe your personal miracle to somebody else. Celebrate together.

4. Answer in writing the questions on the 12 elements of spiritual health in this chapter. When you're finished, reflect over all your answers. Summarize the themes you see in your responses. Share your insights with someone you trust.

# 7

# Putting the Pieces Together
## A Wholistic View

We asked several people to read this far in *The Caring Question* and reflect on their current health status. John answered this way:

> Physically, I'm operating at about 70%. I have lots of energy, but with my sore knee I haven't been able to exercise as I'd like. I'm sleeping well and am relaxed.
>
> Mentally, I'm not very stimulated. I'm bored at work and waiting for a new challenge.
>
> My relationships are so-so. I'm depending on just one person to meet most of my interpersonal needs and I'm not getting much feedback or challenge from anyone.
>
> Spiritually, I'm in super shape! God is at the center of my life and guides my choices. Prayer is a daily solace and resource. I do wonder sometimes, though, if I'm too judgmental.

What about you? How is your health? You may want to leaf through the first half of this book to jog your memory about insights you had while reading. If you took notes or wrote in a journal, scan those as well for your self-care assessment. Then answer the questions below to assess your current health status.

---

### Your Current Health Status Assessment

1. Comment on your current level of health-fullness in all aspects of life. Be very specific. Use examples whenever possible.

Physical Health: I'm

_____

_____

Mental Health: I'm

_____

_____

Relational Health: I'm

_____

_____

Spiritual Health: I'm

_____

_____

2. Fill in the thermometer on page 107 to represent your health-fullness in each of the self-care dimensions.

3. Complete the sentence: I feel most alive when

_____

_____

4. Note anything you would like to change. Aspects of my health I would like to improve:

_____

_____

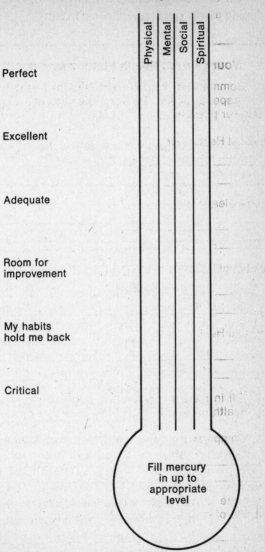

My Health-Fullness
Temperature

Physical  Mental  Social  Spiritual

Perfect

Excellent

Adequate

Room for
improvement

My habits
hold me back

Critical

Fill mercury
in up to
appropriate
level

5. Complete the following statement: If I want my health to improve, I need to stop

_____

and I need to start

_____

I believe this information should be:

_____ ignored        _____ utilized to make changes
                              in my life.

6. Comment on your general satisfaction/dissatisfaction with your total health at this moment.

_____
_____
_____
_____

## WHAT'S YOUR FAVORITE HEALTH FOCUS?

You may have discovered, as John did, that the quality of your health and self-care habits differs among the four dimensions. Rarely do people invest equal amounts of energy in mental, spiritual, relational, and physical health. Each of us determines which aspects are most important to us. We pay special attention to these. One person, for example, might not care much about the ability to think abstractly, but might place high value on physical fitness. Another loves good friends and desires spiritual depth, but doesn't give a hoot about physical conditioning or nutrition.

We all target some aspects of health for special focus, based on our values and priorities. What about you? Is mental health more important to you than spiritual depth? Is physical health more important than friendship? Use the questions below to discover your health-fullness priorities.

Rank each aspect of health in order of its importance to you. Assign #1 to the most important, #2 to the next most important, etc. This forced-choice ranking may be difficult, but it should also help you see what you value in personal health.

_____ Physical Health (strength, energy, freedom from pain, endurance)
_____ Mental Health (memory, humor, good judgment, stability, calmness)
_____ Relational Health (many friends, loving, caring, good contact)
_____ Spiritual Health (peace, hope, confidence, purpose, faith)

What are your highly valued target qualities for health-fullness?

## FAVORITE SYMPTOMS

The health priorities you select determine which symptoms you'll pay attention to and which you'll ignore. Most of us have enough symptoms of ill health to call ourselves sick most of the time. We also have enough signs of wholeness to call ourselves healthy. The symptom you first notice is not necessarily the first that occurs, just the first you're willing to attend to.

Some people get worried about a queasy stomach or changes in their skin long before they even notice the slip in meaningful contact with friends. They're more likely to call a physician for a prescription than a neighbor for coffee and conversation. Other people are particularly attuned to their mood signals so that depression or anxiety is more troublesome to them than arthritis. They can ignore physical pain much more easily than psychic pain.

It's even possible to manipulate symptoms until you

can pick the ones that you want. A father once told us, "My daughter knows that if she's discouraged or worried, she still must go to school, but if she has a high temperature, she can stay home. She can raise her temperature any time she wants to. You know how I know? I used to do it to my mother."

*How about you? If you must experience symptoms of disease in your life, which do you prefer? Which symptoms are least acceptable to you? What will you ignore? And which will cause you to take immediate corrective action?*

## FAVORITE REMEDIES

Your health priorities will also guide your choice of self-care strategies. We all have our favorites and tend to rely on these first, no matter what health problems we face. We each have our own private stock of tried and true remedies for every health dilemma.

If physical exercise generally gets you out of a rut, you'll be likely to try exercise when your body feels tired, when you feel discouraged and empty, or when you can't concentrate anymore. If talking with a friend generally helps you feel better, you're likely to find a friend to talk with, whether your problem is a headache or inability to sleep or loneliness. When you use your old favorites, they're likely to help no matter what's going on. You're comfortable with them, and they "turn you on" again.

The principle of wholeness indicates that the entirety of your health will probably be improved no matter which tried and true remedy you use. So go ahead and use your strengths whenever you can. Just don't limit yourself too narrowly. If your old favorites don't work, try something totally new.

*How about you? List some of your favorite self-care*

*remedies. Are they primarily physical, mental, relational, or spiritual? Which is your all-time favorite remedy—one you fall back on when all else fails? Is your list different than it was five years ago or still essentially the same?*

## MATCH THE REMEDY TO THE SYMPTOM

If your "all-purpose" remedy doesn't work for a particular life situation, how do you choose some other midcourse correction?

We're trained to tackle problems head-on with logic. And the logical place to start would be to select the remedies most likely to relieve the symptoms of discomfort you're experiencing. Here are some of those logical self-care treatments.

**For physical symptoms:** *physical treatment*—exercise, sleep, meditation, change eating, smoking, or drinking habits, relaxation techniques, medication, surgery.

**For mental symptoms:** *mental treatment* — accept yourself, talk with someone, try new behaviors, work on your fears, read, take a course, get more information, analyze your blocks, find new challenges.

**For relational symptoms:** *relational treatment* — find new friends, smile more, give compliments, join an interest group, talk it over, reach out, love, trust.

**For spiritual symptoms:** *spiritual treatment* — prayer, meditation, accept doubts, confess, make a commitment, worship, reflect.

To be sure, the logical approach might lead to a successful strategy for enhancing your health. It's possible, however, that a remedy from a different life dimension would prove to be as effective, or even more effective, than the logical choice.

# TRY A NEW COMBINATION

Since we are whole people, change in any dimension of well-being will affect our overall health. Any strategy we try has a good chance to help us. Could exercise help relieve your feelings of loneliness? Why not! Could prayer help you quit smoking? Maybe so. Check it out for yourself, combine any possible remedies with any symptom, and ask yourself, "Could it help?" You'll probably see that it could.

So you have a problem. You're tired and rundown, or you're feeling pressure at work, or you're worried about a child, or you're depressed and feel empty, or you don't have many friends. What might help?

- An iron supplement?
- Talking with someone who understands?
- Taking your kids fishing?
- Giving out compliments?
- Instituting a lunch hour exercise program?
- Writing in a journal?
- Having an affair with your spouse?
- Focusing on your spiritual development?
- Calling an old friend?
- Volunteering to coach Little League baseball?

Yes, these and thousands of other ideas might be just what you need.

Don't limit yourself to self-care strategies that make "sense." Search out new possibilities in every aspect of life. Try going back to school or springboard diving or values clarification or time management or square dancing or a women's group or evening devotions or a vegetarian diet. Any of these could bring you renewed health and wholeness.

## CREATIVITY CAN MAKE ANY REMEDY MORE EFFECTIVE

No matter what self-care strategy you choose, you can double its effectiveness by adding a creative twist

—and you'll double your enthusiasm for implementing the plan at the same time.

If your relationships need care, you could creatively solicit feedback and challenge. Ask your secretary or your boss to send you a memo every day commenting on some aspect of your work. Ask your spouse to put notes in your lunch or pockets. Organize a feedback exchange with a colleague. Sit with someone new every week at church and ask for their impressions of you. Write a letter to your mother asking her opinion. Put an ad in the paper requesting input from anyone who knows you. Pretend you're writing a creative resume and ask acquaintances for suggestions.

Since your self-care choices are unlimited, don't pick the dull ones. Pick out the ones that turn you on. Choose some crazy, funny, far-out ideas. If they make you laugh, so much the better.

## THE NEXT STEP

Current conventional wisdom dictates that a book about wellness should end here. Most do. We usually think of health as a private, personal matter. This book has covered every aspect of self-care from body to mind to spirit to relationships. We should be finished. So why aren't we at the end?

To stop here could suggest that we believe personal health is an end in itself—a goal for living. On the contrary, we believe that only taking care of yourself—even taking care of your health in all dimensions—is too shallow a goal for health-fullness. What's the point of being well, sitting on a beach, staring at your navel, worshiping yourself?

To keep a healthy balance in life we need to go one step further and ask, "What are you going to do with your health once you get it? What's the purpose of all this self-care?" These questions lead us beyond wellness to the other side of the caring question—care for and commitment to others. Your personal well-being must be used to make a positive difference in your world. People who are truly whole and healthy reach out. How can you reach out with a healthy commitment and purpose? Read on.

## THOUGHT PROVOKERS

### For Individual Reflection and Group Discussion

1. Share your Health Thermometer Readings with others close to you. Ask them how they would have measured your health-fullness in each of the areas based on what they know about you. How can you raise or lower your rating? Do you want to make any changes?

2. Brainstorm all the "sickness" words you can think of in each dimension of life. Try to use at least 20 in each area. We've given you a few to prime the pump:

| Body | Mind | Relationships | Spirit |
|------|------|---------------|--------|
| headache | prejudice | arguments | arrogance |
| fever | depression | rebellion | hopelessness |

What do you see as the common thread in all of these dis-eases?

Now brainstorm all the health-full vocabulary you can think of in each area. Again list at least 20 in each area.

| Body | Mind | Relationships | Spirit |
|------|------|---------------|--------|
| vitality | curious | assertiveness | questions |
| fit | excitement | nurture | faith |

What is the common element in these signs of health? What is the source of healing?

Finally, brainstorm all the remedies available for improving personal health-fullness in each area. List at least 20 in each area.

| Body | Mind | Relationships | Spirit |
|------|------|---------------|--------|
| regular swimming | read a good book | cry with a friend | pray |
| massage | tell a joke | say thank you to someone | watch the sunrise |

Think about your own experience. Select one symptom of a current "sickness" in some dimension of your life. (You may want to choose one from the Body, Mind, Relationships, and Spirit lists above.) Then pick one remedy from each of the four areas of self-care. (Again, use your list of remedies above.) Don't try to make the treatments logical—just choose one from each area that looks interesting. Imagine trying each treatment on your symptom. How would you apply the prescription? What effect do you think it might have? On you? On your symptom? During the next week try the remedies and see what happens.

If you're doing this exercise with a group or your family, let the others help you select "far-out" remedies! See if they can help you add a touch of creativity that could make these odd treatments even more energizing and fun!

3. Describe to others your ranking of the four dimensions of self-care:

- Which aspect of health is most important to you? Least?
- Which symptoms do you attend to? Which do you ignore?
- In which areas of health do you least want symptoms? Which area is preferable if you must have symptoms?

- To which area of self-care do you usually go first to find remedies? Which least? Or never?

Compile a group-average ranking. Then compare yourself with the group norm. Is your pecking order similar to or different from that of others? What does that say about your potential strengths and weaknesses in self-care practices?

# PART 2
## REACHING OUT

# 8

# Being "Well-to-Do"
## The Reach-Out Dimension

---

**BORED MILLIONAIRES
BUY A STORE**

SHEFFIELD, England—George and Elaine Dawes are buying a sporting goods store. They got bored at having nothing to do after winning a $1.8 million lottery jackpot.

"We don't want to be idle for the rest of our lives," George Dawes told reporters Sunday.

After their big win last year for guessing the results of soccer matches, the couple stopped working. George Dawes, 39, gave up his job as a salesman and his wife, 37, closed down her neighborhood general store.

They bought a luxury house with a swimming pool and a Rolls-Royce and took holidays in the Caribbean, the Mediterranean, and Europe.

"Now we are looking forward to getting up early in the morning once again," Elaine Dawes said.

---

Every one of us needs a reason to get up in the morning. What's yours? You want to make something of yourself? You want to stack up enough money so you and your family will be secure no matter what happens to the economy? You want the freedom to take exotic vacations? You want to be more successful than your neighbors and friends? If so, like this couple, one morning you're likely to wake up aching with emptiness. Money, freedom, fancy toys, and exotic vacations are not enough to sustain us day after day.

We all need a reason, a good reason, to get up in the morning. Taking care of our own needs, desires, and wishes won't sustain us for long. Good self-care habits give us the ability to respond to others. This responseability must be exercised, or it withers—and with it we shrivel too. To be truly healthy we need to focus on purposes beyond ourselves. Service to people and causes outside ourselves gives us the energy for tackling another day.

## THE POWER OF PURPOSE

Author Gail Sheehy interviewed hundreds of people across the country who were recommended to her as models of success. Their answers to one key question separated the true pathfinders from their self-centered look-alikes. The question? "Are you devoted to some purpose or cause outside of yourself and larger than yourself?" Astonishingly, most answered no. Sheehy soon discovered that these models of success were, in fact, completely engrossed with themselves and that most had left behind a carnage of injured family, friends, and colleagues on their way to the top. True pathfinders, on the other hand, answered the question with a resounding yes! They, like we, believe that health involves reaching out, even at cost to self. People stay healthy when life makes sense to them. Commitment to a purpose larger than ourselves gives us that meaning.

*What about you? After you dig under your flip fantasies of fame, power, and fortune, what purposes for living lure you out of bed morning after morning? On what people and what purposes larger than yourself are you focused? Your love of your children? Your desire to make the world a better place for them to live? Your conviction that war is immoral? Your plan to alleviate some human suffering each day? Your sense of responsibility to your parents? Your loyalty to your friends? Your faith in education? Your sacrifice for your spouse? What positive difference are you trying to make in your world? To what are you committed?*

## THE COMMITMENT CHALLENGE

These are tough questions. Making commitments is demanding. Why? First, because we have to make decisions. With only a limited amount of time and energy we can't commit ourselves to everyone and every cause. We must make choices—difficult choices. Second, reaching out will cost us something. At times we'll have to sacrifice ourselves, putting our own needs and desires aside for the moment in order to focus first on giving others what they need. Third, it's risky. The results of our efforts are never certain. We can never know ahead of time whether our self-sacrifice will make a positive difference. Making commitments on how to spend ourselves for others takes determined, gritty effort.

Paul and Sarah Goodman know this decision-making process well. Years ago they made a commitment to keep their family life central. They shared the belief that parenting was a top priority and discussed the issue at length, even before marriage. As their four children have grown through adolescence, their commitment to the family has been affirmed and reaffirmed, made and remade over and over again.

The Goodmans' investment in parenting has carried a high price tag. Over the years Paul and later Sarah have taken on stimulating careers. But the Goodmans have never allowed their careers to eat up family time. Family friendships take precedence over the pursuit of friendships that exclude children. Leisurely vacations as a couple have been replaced by hectic, inexpensive camping trips with the kids. Sleep, once lost for sick children, is now interrupted by calls from stranded kids or crack-of-dawn chauffeuring. Any extra money goes for musical instruments or the kids' education funds rather than for luxuries for parents. Do the Goodmans complain about the cost of this sacrifice? Absolutely not!

Like all parents, the Goodmans have no guarantee that their children will turn out the way they imagine and hope. Paul and Sarah know their limitations and affirm their own efforts: "We took our best shot at it. Now we'll just have to see."

Fred and Sue Morris made a commitment as well. Solid, midwestern beef-eaters, they chose several years ago to become vegetarians—not for food preference or health reasons, but on principle. "Since so much of the world is hungry," they reasoned, "we should eat lower on the food chain. If everyone did so, there would be enough food for all." Every day they pay for that decision. Neighbors and friends don't understand. Meal preparation takes more time. Eating out is nearly impossible. And, what's more, they both still like meat. Will the Morrises' commitment to this principle make the world a better place? Will it influence others? They hope so, but don't know. Fred and Sue accept the cost of their cause with no guarantees of success.

Such is the nature of any commitment. Anytime we reach out, we make a choice from among many options. That choice carries the cost of self-sacrifice, and its results are never guaranteed.

## MAKING HEALTH-FULL INVESTMENTS

We believe commitment to service that focuses on giving rather than receiving, characterized by the repeated choice to reach out and love, is an essential element in wholeness. You cannot be health-full unless you reach out. Whole people are "well-to-*do*."

In the next chapters we'll focus on three arenas for making commitments: family, "neighbors," and creation. Before you go on to explore your commitments in these areas, please take a moment to ponder your present priorities. The quiz below will give you some idea of your current outreach patterns.

---

### Outreach Inventory

| Yes | No | Family |
|-----|-----|--------|
| \_\_\_\_ | \_\_\_\_ | Staying in touch with my extended family is a top priority for me. |
| \_\_\_\_ | \_\_\_\_ | I readily accept the responsibility to care for dependent family members who are less able than I because of age, health, or abilities. |
| \_\_\_\_ | \_\_\_\_ | I hug all members of my family regularly and directly communicate my caring for them in other ways. |
| \_\_\_\_ | \_\_\_\_ | I have said no to stimulating life options in order to care for my family. For periods of time I have made the family's welfare more important than my own. |

_____ _____ I find it possible to accept and affirm each family member as he or she is, complete with strengths and weaknesses, beauty and blemishes.

_____ _____ I regularly participate in family time: special rituals, celebrations, and traditions that promote communication and a positive history.

*Note:* Complete only one of the next two sections—whichever applies to you.

Yes    No              *For Singles Only*

_____ _____ I accept myself as a single person and believe that God accepts me and my feelings.

_____ _____ I live in the "now" as a single, free to be me rather than yearning for a past or future partner.

_____ _____ I am clear about who I am, my purpose in life and my values.

_____ _____ I search for intimacy in the context of my personal guidelines for responsible sexuality.

_____ _____ I am assertive about filling my calendar and my life with meaningful relationships and activities.

_____ _____ I am committed to at least one project that will improve the quality of life for someone else.

Yes    No              *For Marrieds Only*

_____ _____ I give compliments to my spouse several times each day and frequently express genuine gratitude.

_____ _____ I share feelings of anger and frustration directly with my spouse and attempt to resolve conflicts.

_____ _____ I frequently reaffirm my commitment to my spouse and periodically clarify and renegotiate the details of our covenant with him/her.

_____ _____ I set aside time regularly, as well as on special occasions, for my spouse and me to invest in our caring relationship.

_____ _____ I forgive my spouse readily and without resentment.

_____ _____ I am willing to postpone the fulfillment of some of my needs and my dreams for myself in order to allow my spouse to be more fulfilled.

*Yes    No*          *"Neighbors"*

_____ _____ I respect others for their uniqueness and do not find it necessary to try to make them be like me.

_____ _____ I try to personally touch each person I meet each day with kindness and warmth.

_____ _____ I practice being attentive to the needs of others around me — even if they're not spoken. I'm willing to bear others' burdens in any way I can.

_____ _____ I am a good listener and can listen empathically without judgment.

_____ _____ I volunteer to share my gifts for the good of others both in my close neighborhood and beyond.

_____ _____ I tell others what I appreciate about them.

*Yes    No*          *Creation*

_____ _____ I am committed to a cause beyond myself, and I invest some of my money, my time, and my energy in it.

_____ _____ I feel compassion for all and I feel pain whenever anyone is put down or held back because of their race, sex, or religious views. Whenever I see this occur, I speak up.

_____ _____ I try to consume only what I need and take pride in moving through the world lightly and living simply. My life is not overburdened with "things."

_____ _____ I feel personally responsible to keep the environment clean, often stopping to pick up cans, wrappers, etc.

_____ _____ I have a balanced perspective on the purpose and use of money and do not stack it up for its own sake.

_____ _____ I am determined that because I am here, this world will be a better place to live than it would have been without me.

Count up your yes responses for each category and record them below.

| | | |
|---|---|---|
| Family | _____ | Yes responses |
| Singles or Marrieds | _____ | Yes responses |
| Neighbors | _____ | Yes responses |
| Creation | _____ | Yes responses |
| Total | _____ | Yes responses |

## HOW TO INTERPRET YOUR SCORE

Your total yes answers on the Outreach Inventory provides you with an indication of your investments in service and self-sacrifice. Compare your total score with the Caring Question Standards.

21-24   Excellent:   You're obviously intent on making a positive difference in your world.

12-19   Average:   You do reach out, but you might consider expanding your reach.

Below 12   Poor:   You're in danger of being self-engrossed.

For specifics on your self-sacrifice patterns, pay particular attention to your score in each of the categories. Your answers indicate your priorities. Did you total very few yes responses in one category but many in another? Where are your strengths in reaching out? Where are your weaknesses?

Obviously, you can't reach out everywhere at once. Do your answers adequately reflect your values? Is any adjustment needed? If you recorded three or fewer yes responses in any category, you may be neglecting your responsibility to reach out in that area.

## REFLECTIONS

Take a few minutes to reflect on your outreach score and your reactions to it. Use the worksheet below to record your insights and any resolutions for change.

---

### Personal Reflections on My Well-to-Do Pattern

In what areas are your current outreach investments adequate?

---

In which areas are you neglecting your responsibility?

---

Note your reactions:

---

In which areas would you like to increase or decrease your investment of self?

---

Which specific habits would you like to modify?

---

As you explore your options for reaching out in the next four chapters, affirm your strengths and focus on those areas where you'd like to improve. Then share your reactions with someone you love.

# THOUGHT PROVOKERS

## For Individual Reflection and Group Discussion

1. Make a diagram showing your purpose-in-life time line. Recall the first time you can remember being aware of a purpose outside yourself (wanting to help a blind person cross the street, giving a gift to your mom). From that point chart your growth in sense of purpose over the years.

- What twists and turns has the line taken as you've opened some doors in commitment and closed others in surrender?
- Have there been dry spells? Show them.
- Label the turning points (confirmation, work camp, divorce), the difficult choices, the changing purposes (draft resistance, right to life), the new investments.
- Extend your purpose line into the future, predicting what growth looms ahead for you.

Share your time line with your parents or someone who knows you very well. Can that person describe your journey from the diagram alone?

- Trade time lines with someone else in your group.
- After studying the diagram for a few minutes, do your best to introduce that person to the group by describing two of the life purposes.

2. Imagine that you suddenly inherit a million dollars.

- What might you do with the money?
- What dreams would you fulfill? Be as specific as possible.
- Make up a tentative budget that accounts for all the money (travel, books, recreation, savings, investment, contributions, etc.).
- Compare notes with others in your group.

How do you imagine your life might change with such a nest egg?

- What in your present life-style would you not want changed or disrupted?

If you had all the money you needed, why would you get up in the morning?

- When?
- What would you try to accomplish with your day?
- Would you have a purpose outside yourself?

3. Summarize and discuss with others the results of your Outreach Inventory. Listen to their stories and try to become aware of how each has chosen unique individual patterns for reaching out. Can you learn anything from the style of others that prompts you to revise or reaffirm your outreach commitment?

# 9

# **Charity Begins at Home**
## Reach Out to Your Family

Most people belong to two families during their lifetime—the family they are born into and live with during childhood and the one they create when they marry and have children of their own. In both of these families, commitment is the glue that holds them together over time. The repeated decision to stick together through the best and worst of times, to care for one another, and to sacrifice when necessary for the common good—these are the essence of family. When people reach out to one another with this commitment, the family becomes a valuable health resource for its members.

In our society, families function as the primary nurturing network. Within the context of the family we give and receive the emotional support that nourishes our sense of self and satisfies many interpersonal needs. We share touch and physical tenderness. In the family setting we learn to experience and express our feelings, to respect and trust others, and to care for ourselves. The rituals and celebrations of family life provide focus for our spiritual growth and development as well.

In short, the family provides a crucible for pursuing the health and wholeness we've been examining in the first half of this book. It is also within the family that we learn about the health-fullness of reaching out to care for others.

## REACHING OUT IN THE FAMILY

In our "first family" our parents may have taken care of us, but as we grow into adulthood the care-giving changes direction. Whether we marry and start our own family of choice or remain single, we find ourselves on the other side of the giving/getting equation. Suddenly we become the nurturers rather than the nurtured. Our attention shifts from taking care of ourselves to putting others' needs first. Each time we choose to care for our family, even when we don't really feel like it, we forfeit immediate rewards in favor of long-term gains.

Self-denial and self-sacrifice come with the territory. You sacrifice for your children, for your parents, for your partner. You offer whatever is needed regardless of the cost because you believe that the other person's welfare is equally important and sometimes even more important than your own. What parent wouldn't sacrifice a night's sleep to care for a sick child?

Martha and Ryan Riley discovered surprising new depths of caring and commitment in themselves with the birth of their first child, Sean. Neither of these two very independent adults was prepared for the sacrifices demanded by the responsibility to care for this infant. The luxuries of their former child-free life-style disappeared overnight. Extra time and money to spend alone or as a couple, control over the day's schedule, leisurely evenings of intimacy are all now a thing of the past. In spite of all the adjustments, the Rileys agree that Sean is the best thing that ever happened to them. Both Ryan and Martha have stretched their personal limits and experienced the joy of reaching out in ways they never imagined before.

We believe that this kind of reaching out in commitment to family is essential to health-fullness. As we give ourselves to others we grow in caring, tolerance, and understanding. Our investment gives us the opportunity to live within limits and for a purpose beyond ourselves.

*What about you? How much of your time and energy do you invest in your families? What sacrifices do you make to honor these commitments? What healthy benefits do you receive?*

## MAKE THE FAMILY TOP PRIORITY

What does it take to create a healthy family? Family researcher David Olson discovered that for a family to function well its members must be adaptable enough to solve problems and to share roles when necessary. Families also require a bond of togetherness and shared experience strong enough to sustain them during periods of strain or crisis. Families with a good balance of flexibility and commitment provide a healthy environment for their members.

We take this definition of a healthy family one step further. The healthiest families we've encountered have one other characteristic in common: they make deliberate decisions to invest time and energy in their relationships. They make family a number one priority.

The Goodmans we met in the last chapter are a good example of this. They decided to make their children top priority. So Paul and Sarah are involved in their children's lives and are interested in them as people. Children need that kind of attention from parents. The healthiest families provide the most love and concern for their children.

Keeping the family as a top priority helps us decide on how to invest our limited resources. When the children are still at home, that's the time to choose outside activities that include the family: to be a Scout leader or work with the PTA, to plan family outings and activities, to connect with other families whose children mesh with yours. Later in life you'll have time to involve yourself elsewhere. If you throw yourself into too many activities away from home, you may not have the reserves you need to deal with all the predictable and unpredictable crises that come along with childrearing.

Healthy outreach also extends beyond the boundaries of the nuclear family. Including Grandma in your outing to the 4th of July parade or a piano recital affirms your commitment to family. So what if she dresses in strange clothing and talks too loud—she's still family! Spending the weekend with your brother and his family, even when few of your needs get met in the interaction, can be a healthy outreach as well.

Living in a family teaches us about accepting limitations—our own and others. We don't have much choice about who's a part of our family, so we learn to love (or put up with) all kinds of people of all ages. You can't disown Cousin Bess just because she's a prig. You don't ostracize your sister because she has a cleft palate. You don't snub your father-in-law when he's forgetful. Neither do the others in your family discount you because you have buck teeth or an offbeat sense of humor.

*What about you? Where does family fit in your priorities? How satisfied are you with your relationships to extended family? Are there any family members with whom you need to mend fences?*

There's something intrinsically healthy about being part of a family and staying in touch with its multiple generations. Make your family a top priority. Stay in touch with round-robin letters, bargain-time phone calls, or frequent reunions.

## EXPANDING THE FAMILY MEMORY BANK

Build a sense of family history and continuity by spending time together filling the family memory bank. Every family has a storehouse of collective memories. "Remember the year we went to Yellowstone and the tent almost blew over?" "Remember the time we got stuck in the elevator?" "Remember the blizzard of '66?" "Remember the 21-gun salute at Grandpa's funeral?" "Remember when Chuck fell off his bike?" "Remember Cousin Beth's wedding?" "Remember Mom and Dad's 40th-anniversary surprise party?"

Recalling peak experiences, reliving familiar rituals and traditions, and retelling family stories keeps the family connected and its spirit alive. The Rileys started their memory bank when Sean was born. They created a pictorial essay from conception to delivery. Every year since, on his birthday, Martha and Ryan use the photo album to retell the story for Sean. They've added many other shared experiences to their memory bank, but they treasure this ritual the most.

*What about you? What traditions and memories remind you of your commitment to family? What could you do to expand your family memory bank?*

# A LESSON FROM THE OYSTER

Not all family memory boxes are filled with pleasant images. Some are crowded with nightmares of pain or anger or loneliness or conflict. Life in a family is often the pits rather than a bowl of cherries. With children you inherit crises—health problems, behavior problems, difficulties at school, conflicts with friends, handicaps, or rebellion—along with no guarantees for success in resolving them. Our commitment to one another in the family provides the context for working out, rather than walking away from, the problems.

Consider the oyster. When a grain of sand sneaks into its shell, it irritates the muscle. To defend itself the oyster sacrifices some of its own tissue to smooth over the troublesome sand, adding layer after layer until a pearl is formed.

All families have problems—some more than others. When we reach out like the oyster and carefully give of ourselves to smooth things over, we turn our problems into pearls. All kinds of events and situations disrupt the family. Few solutions, of course, are as permanent as the pearl. Part of our commitment to family is the resolution to keep looking for alternative solutions when the current approach isn't working.

Sometimes the solution may require letting go and letting be. If your teenage daughter is determined to hang around with a group of friends you consider undesirable, you may not be able to control the situation. After exploring other options you may eventually have to let go and say, "It's out of my control."

Some problems may need the intervention of someone outside the family. If you've exhausted your resources as a family for dealing with your toddler's temper tantrums, your family might seek out a counselor for assistance.

*What about you? What difficulties in your family need smoothing over? What have you done to help your family live with the problem?*

## FINDING THE FORGIVENESS FACTOR

What happens in a family when problems don't get solved? When people are angry with one another? Or envious? When people hurt or misunderstand each other?

Families need some way to reach out to one another with love and forgiveness. Most of us haven't had much experience with true forgiveness. We need to learn how to ask for, grant, and accept forgiveness.

Where do you start when your spouse makes fun of you in public? When you've jumped on your kids for something petty? When your mother flies off the handle? When your daughter is caught shoplifting? When you and your brother have a big argument? When your partner turns away from your request for lovemaking? How do you give and receive forgiveness in the family?

The starting point is to acknowledge that forgiveness is not a feeling, it's a choice. It's actually two choices—the decision made by one person to repent and the decision made by the other to forgive. When you've done something for which you need forgiveness, admit it. Swallow your pride, take the risk, and make your request directly to the injured person: "Steve, will you forgive me? I really hurt you, and I'm sorry." This kind of direct request gives the other person the chance to say, "Yes, I forgive you," rather than retaliate. It also provides a wonderful model for others in the family to imitate.

When others wrong you, choose to forgive them as God has freely forgiven you. If you can let go of your righteous indignation when you've been hurt, you'll go a long way toward bringing the forgiveness factor to life in your family.

Forgiveness is not forgetting; it's refusing to hold grudges. Forgiveness doesn't demand that the other change first. Forgiveness is an attitude freely given that accepts hurts and drops the charges. We believe that forgiveness is one of the most health-full ways to reach out to those you love.

Because we live so closely together in the family, our relationships are punctuated by conflict and accented by strong feeling. How do we build bridges in place of walls? How do we repair broken promises? How do we rebuild trust? How do we heal violated relationships? Every family needs mechanisms for forgiveness so that it can start over fresh—again and again. Seek out and practice a variety of rituals for asking and offering forgiveness in your family.

*What about you? What's the forgiveness factor in your family? Which transgressions are the hardest for you to forgive? In what ways do you avoid asking for or offering direct forgiveness? What forgiveness rituals might work well for you?*

## ACCENTUATE THE POSITIVE

It's all too easy to get caught in the habit of being critical and judgmental of others, especially those in our family. Parents may offer a constant stream of directions or prohibitions: "Please unload the dishwasher," "Stop making that noise," "Pick up your toys!," "Don't be late!," "When are you going to get your practicing done?" Or they give lots of unsolicited feedback, "Your hair needs washing," "That blouse doesn't go with that jumper," "You need to spend more time on your homework," "Wear a belt." Is this the kind of care-full reaching out that promotes health for both giver and receiver? We think not.

Why not replace these negative health habits with a focus on what we appreciate about the members of our family? The most wonderful gift we can give to one another is affirmation. Try these suggestions sometime soon.

**Say I love you.** When was the last time you professed your love to your father? To your brother? To your child? How often do you let your family members know you care about them? Four times a day? Four times a week? Four times a year? Never, because you assume they already know?

Don't delegate this powerful gift. Don't assume that others know you care. Don't be stingy with your love. Tell your family you love them with your words, with your looks, with your touch, with your attitude, with your thoughtfulness—several times a day!

**Affirm one another.** Focus on each individual in your family and identify several qualities that make that person unique. Tell each what you appreciate as special about him or her. Affirm your child or your partner or your daughter-in-law for her attitude, for a particular skill, for a task well done, for a smile. None of us ever gets enough of this special brand of caring.

One wise mother we know shared her secret of success. "I've never said this out loud before," she told us, "but one of my guiding principles in raising a family has been to treat each member with as much courtesy, respect, and interest as I would a guest." Judging by the obvious love, the positive spirit, and the vibrant health of her family, her strategy has worked wonders.

The family is our most intense context for practicing the health-full art of reaching out to care for others. Although the costs of sacrifice may at times seem to outweigh the rewards, your investment of yourself over time will bring you a richness and depth found no other way.

## REFLECTIONS

Before we move on to explore the caring question from the single person's perspective, please take a few minutes to reflect on your patterns of reaching out to your family. Do your family behaviors enhance or erode your health-fullness?

---

### Personal Reflections on My Outreach to Family

My family as priority (children, parents, grandparents, choices I make)

_____

_____

Problem-solving patterns (methods for smoothing things out, reaction to disagreements, to hurts)

_____

_____

My forgiveness behavior (asking for forgiveness, offering forgiveness, meaningful rituals)

_____

_____

My affirmation of family (memory bank, sense of history, affirmation of each member).

_____

_____

### Wish List for Health-Fullness

List here everything you can imagine wanting in your outreach to your family. What would you be able to *do*? To *feel*? Let your imagination run free. Don't limit yourself in any way. The wishes don't have to be practical.

I wish I could:

_____

_____

_____

## THOUGHT PROVOKERS

### For Individual Reflection and Group Discussion

1. Draw a picture of your family with you in it. Use symbols or words or colors to show the connections between members. What signs of health and unhealth do you see in your family portrait?

Share your drawing with the rest of the family and discuss ways you all could make an even more healthy investment in each other.

Did you include any member of your extended family in your picture? Why? Why not? How do they, or don't they, fit into your family?

2. List some of the spoken and unspoken rules in your family that govern conduct and relationships ("Don't talk about our family with others," "We must always stick together," "Never talk back to your parents").

- Have any of these rules changed over the years?
- Are the rules the same in your family of choice as they were in your family of origin?
- How has your family been affected by these rules?
- Which are you convinced are essential? Which could be modified or dropped?
- What happens when someone in the family doesn't follow the rules?

How does your family deal with personal limitations, mistakes, transgressions of rules? How does your family deal with family problems that involve everyone?

How does your family announce forgiveness to each other? With your family or group develop a forgiveness/acceptance ritual that you can use during difficult times.

3. Make a list of the five most positive experiences in your family memory bank. Spend a few minutes recalling the details of each experience.

- What happened? How? What did it mean?
- What did you learn?
- How does the strength of this experience still contribute to your family today?

Share these experiences with others.

This week sit down with your family (or call on the phone) and speak a direct and special "I love you" by telling each family member what you especially appreciate about his or her contribution to your family memory bank.

# 10

# On Your Own
## Reach Out as a Single

So, you're single. Congratulations! You're presented with unique opportunities to reach out. Condolences! You're also faced with predictable pitfalls. Whether you're single by chance or by choice, your life position is a mixed bag of banes and blessings.

Plenty of problems can crop up when you're living single in a couple-focused world, especially if you're not single by preference.

- What do you do with the hurt feelings, the anger, the grief, and the fear? Or about your sense of guilt and failure? Or questions of self-worth? Or jealousy or loneliness?
- How do you make and keep friends? And be open and intimate without driving others away? What do you say when you don't want to be sexually intimate, but do want to keep dating? How do you relate with married friends? How and where do you meet new people who stimulate you? Who can you share your day with? Your joys and your sorrows?
- How do you raise your children on your own? Can you really be both mother and father? What about times

when you feel overwhelmed with no one else to share the decisions, the joys, the burdens?

• Where do you find enough money to pay all the bills? Why must you hassle to get credit?

• Is there any church not focused mainly on couples with children? Where can you find one that gives more than lip service to singles issues—one where you will feel at home and accepted?

• What is your purpose? Who are you? Where are you going? What do you want?

There are plenty of questions about single life in this society, and no easy answers.

Is it any wonder? Our society offers few rules for being a responsible "well-to-*do*" single, and fewer models. Many who find themselves suddenly single are unprepared for the uncharted territory they've entered. It seems like a foreign country with a different language and strange social guidelines. In response, many are caught in the common traps of the single existence. Then, unable to reach out, they withdraw into themselves.

## FOUR COMMON SINGLE TRAPS

**Isolating yourself for protection.** The repetitious cycle of new names and faces, one-time meetings, relationships with promise, dashed hopes, and loneliness wears down one's social courage. Meeting, relating, investing, then divesting—over and over again in a sputtering, inconsistent rhythm—is physically and mentally exhausting. It can lead to misunderstandings, hurt feelings, confusion, loss of confidence, fear of reaching out, and negativism. It's tough to keep starting over and over again and again.

Adopting a cautious, even calloused attitude may appear to be wise self-defense. It's tempting to pull back, start worrying about self, become self-centered, and end up withdrawn, isolated, and stagnant. Tempting, but hardly a rewarding position. Hardly a posture from which to reach out. A surefire antidote for the isolation trap is the continued courage to risk being vulnerable—no matter what!

**Viewing single life as a temporary holding pattern.** After an initial period of intense grief, widowed and divorced persons often find themselves living in a holding pattern, unable or unwilling to see themselves as single adults. Never-marrieds often spend years after college thinking of themselves as recent graduates waiting for their real life to begin after marriage. This mind-set makes it impossible to get on with life. Everything seems temporary and disconnected. You may say to yourself, "This is not life. This is not me. I'm waiting—waiting until this temporary state of singleness is over and I can get on with my life again."

Unfortunately, this attitude leaves you in a holding pattern—flying around in circles going nowhere until you can land. It's as if you say to yourself, "The past may be real, the future is real, but *now*—now is just waiting until this singleness phase of life is over."

Looking for a spouse is not a rewarding focus for life. It colors every encounter—every social occasion, project, job, friendship—it colors life with disappointment each time you recognize that you haven't found Prince Charming or Miss America after all.

This roller coaster of anticipation and frustration will keep hurling you up and down unless you decide, "OK, I'm single. That's me, and I'll now get on with my life as a single." Until you accept yourself as a single person and admit that this life position might be permanent, you can't really get on with making personal commitments to be who you are and to make a full investment of yourself in your world.

The best medicine for this "temporary insanity" is an attitude shift. Tell yourself, "Life is now! I'd best get on with deciding who I am and living my own life as a single adult."

**Wandering in a spiritual wilderness.** For some, single life is like being lost in unfamiliar territory without map or compass. Being on your own without parents or spouse to define you and tell you what to do can be devastating as well as liberating. Given a chance, perhaps for the first time, to discover your own style and identity, you may ask the question, "Who am I?"—and come up with no answers or too many answers.

It's hard to maintain a steady course when you have no permanent roots, few personal rules of conduct, no routines to depend on, and no one to be responsible for. With too few or too many dreams and no clear goals, it's easy to wander in circles.

Those who attempt to negotiate the daily decisions of living without personal guidelines and a firm sense of their own identity often end up making idols of their own immediate needs, getting for themselves whatever they can, wherever they find it. It's tempting to replace committed companionships with random sexual contact. Spiritual growth sits on the back burner. Meaningful outreach becomes difficult if not impossible.

If wandering in the wilderness is one of your single traps, your own internal wisdom can give you direction. Meaning, purpose, and personal guidelines are found only within. Seek out your own identity and get to know yourself as you grow.

**Struggling with the friendship dilemma.** Everyone needs the care, warmth, shared history, and mutual exchange of friendship. Many people learn little in their lifetime about the process of cultivating friendships, depending instead on social conventions and institutional settings to automatically provide their companions.

Previously married singles are often surprised by the necessity for actively seeking out friends and developing skills of friendship they'd not had to think about before. When your spouse is no longer available to be supportive, to listen to the day's stories, to share in the dishes, to make a cup of coffee, and to plan weekend activities, whom do you turn to? How can you find friends to share in your day-to-day life?

Friendship in the singles world presents a double bind. On the one hand, "no commitment" is the norm. Many singles want relationships with no strings attached ("We'll enjoy ourselves now, but I'm not getting tied down"). On the other hand, the real, sustained, vitalizing intimacy that all of us yearn for is possible only when commitment is present in a relationship—when two people can depend on each other for care whenever needed.

How can you form strong bonds of friendship without the continuity of frequent day-to-day contact? How can you behave with openness, warmth, and sparkle without being interpreted as sexually inviting? How can you pursue the intimacy of close familiarity, sharing of frustrations and fears, and mutual support in a world that defines intimacy as sexual contact? How can you continue friendships with married couples when their focus and priorities are so different—and sexual overtones and jealousy often creep in? How can you find friends of your own faith in churches that treat singleness as an abnormality or temporary handicap? How can you deal with jealousy, misunderstanding, and anger when you or someone else in your circle is left out, either by accident or on purpose?

Friendship in the singles world poses tough challenges. The only sure way to avoid the struggle is to withdraw. If you don't try reaching out in friendship, you won't have to face the possible overtones, fears, and hurt feelings. You may successfully dodge the dilemma, but in the process you lose all opportunity for forming deep and satisfying relationships.

If you want to tackle the friendship dilemma head-on, choose your own special way to care and then care like crazy. Don't get down on yourself when someone betrays your trust. Keep reaching out and risking in your own committed way as best you are able. Know when to let go of unfulfilling relationships to allow yourself more energy to cultivate nurturing friendships.

## REFLECTIONS

How about you? How have you experienced the traps of being single?

---

Have you ever withdrawn and isolated yourself from the single jungle for self-protection?
- In what ways?
- For how long
- With what effect?
- How has this stopped you from reaching out to others?

Have you been enticed into seeing your life as a holding pattern and been caught waiting for the time when your "real" life would begin again?
- What specific attitudes colored your perspective?
- How do you feel about seeking a spouse? What effect does this have on your life-style?
- How has this stopped you from reaching out to others?

When have you felt like you were wandering in a spiritual wilderness?
- What roots have you discarded?
- What rules of conduct have you altered?
- What responsibilities to others have you dropped?

- What dreams have you lost?
- How has this stopped you from reaching out to others?

How have you experienced the dilemma of friendships in the singles world?
- What interpersonal skills did you need to dust off?
- What risks have you taken?
- What disappointments have you experienced?
- What misunderstandings have occurred?
- What effect have these experiences had on you?
- How have they stopped you from reaching out to others?

Have you experienced any other traps of the single life that make you want to flinch and withdraw? How have you handled them?

---

No single person is totally untouched by the dilemma of living as a single in our family-focused society. But most survive the pressures very well and successfully find ways to reach out creatively to touch others in their world. You do have to reach out to others; being single doesn't allow you to escape that responsibility. Here are some ideas for escaping the traps, taking charge, and reaching out that have worked well for others.

## HINTS ON HOW TO REACH OUT

**Accept your feelings.** Feelings are part of life, an important part for everyone. Without the comforting buffer of a constant companion, singles experience feelings of loneliness, fear, hurt, and despair in a raw form. Often they must deal with these emotions alone, and the feelings seem almost overwhelming.

As tough as they may seem, these feelings are natural and normal. Don't deny them or try to change them. Learn to accept them and live with them. When your feelings seem overwhelming, listen to them and note that you do indeed live through them and regain your spirit and willingness to invest yourself in others.

Try to accept yourself as you are—and let God accept you as you feel. It's the first step in preparing to reach out to your world.

**Develop your identity and end the holding pattern.** It's scary to ask "Who am I?" and to come up with no answers. It's also an opportunity. You are free to choose *what you want to be*. Wake up to the fact that the life you're living right now is your life. Don't waste perfectly good years waiting. Choose your way of investing yourself now. You now have opportunities you may not have had in the past and might not have in the future. Take advantage of them.

Take time to test out new elements in your identity. Find out whether you can be a competent business person, a handy fixer, a decorator, a care receiver, or care giver—whatever you've always wanted to be. See what new images of yourself you enjoy.

Take time to center yourself and discover your purpose. Grow in faith. Discover the difference you want to make in your world, and how you want to represent yourself to others. Your life is *now*.

**Confront the friendship dilemma.** In spite of the difficulty you may experience in forming meaningful and lasting friendships, keep on investing yourself. Although you can't control the responses people make to your efforts, you can control your own behavior. Be the kind of person you want to be.

Be honest. Risk. Make yourself vulnerable. Some people will respond, some won't. Experiment with sharing difficult feelings that may lead to intimacy, rather than running away when a relationship gets too close or demanding. Make a commitment to reach out and care for others, even when it costs you or they don't reciprocate. Practice trusting and investing again.

Clarify your personal rules for responsible sexuality and stick with your own guidelines. Whether your rules are "never" or "never again" or "only when I really care" or "whenever it seems like fun," you can still participate responsibly. Responsible sexuality must include care for yourself, gentleness and sensitivity to others, and respect for the relationship. Without these three ingredients any sexual decision you make will be irresponsible and damaging to someone.

As difficult as it is to build the kind of friendships you need, work at it regularly. Find your style of reaching out with care and touching others with your love.

**Be assertive in making plans.** The happiest singles are those who make plans several times each week to get together with others. These vital singles are usually open and let others know they can call for help with a problem or for just plain companionship. You can be the catalyst who sets up creative occasions that you and others look forward to with high anticipation.

The singles who are most miserable sit at home passively waiting for the phone to ring, thinking, "Poor me! Does anyone care about me? I wonder if my friends have forgotten about me again. Don't they know I'm lonely?" No one can read your mind, so don't expect them to.

Set up occasions that fill your needs for contact with others. If you don't like social occasions at bars, or large cocktail parties, set up something more meaningful such as a sharing/support group, or a service project helping those less fortunate. Be assertive. Dial your phone and make something positive happen for you and for others.

**Reach out to your extended family.** Rather than viewing the demands of your extended family as burdens, relabel them as opportunities. Others in your family may still need you. Call or write letters. Set up evenings to share feelings with your children, your parents, your siblings, your cousins, aunts and uncles, nieces and nephews. Lean on one another for support when you need it. Let your children draw you outside of yourself. And if blood relatives aren't available or receptive, adopt some "soul relatives" as your family and reach out to them.

**Carefully choose projects and causes as caring commitments.** You can reach out to your world in your vocation or job. You can reach out through your outside involvements and avocations.

Since you don't have a spouse and may not have children to focus on, set up your life so you can reach out in other ways. Get together with people who are lonely or hurting, volunteer to lead spiritual retreats, coach a drill team, work for worldwide peace, or deliver meals on wheels to the elderly.

Sure, you are busy trying to keep your own life together, but don't kid yourself that you have absolutely no time at all. Find some way to reach out that fits the time and energy you do have. Make sure that some people's lives are different because of your efforts. Reach out beyond yourself, your family, or your friends—into the wider world.

## REFLECTIONS

Before we move on to look at the caring question in marriage, please take a few minutes to reflect on your reach-out patterns as a single. Do they enhance or erode your health-fullness?

## Personal Reflections on My
## Reaching Out as a Single

Accepting my own feelings (grief, fear, loneliness, hurt, etc.)

_____

_____

Ending the holding pattern and developing my own identity (who I am, what I'm trying to be and do with my life, my centering and spiritual growth patterns)

_____

_____

My friendship behavior (honesty, risk, intimacy, trust—with men and with women; my sexual responsibility; my efforts at being a friend and developing friendships)

_____

_____

My assertiveness and creativity in making people plans (being available to help, calling others, setting up creative ways to meet)

_____

_____

My outreach to family (contact with relatives, attitude toward their expectations, extending my family, adopting others)

_____

_____

My caring commitments (through my work, my use of personal time, my use of money, my offering of skills, my caring in organized ways)

_____

_____

## Wish List for Health-Fullness

List here everything you can imagine wanting in your outreach as a single person. What would you be able to *do*? To *feel*? Let your imagination run free. Don't limit yourself in any way. The wishes don't have to be practical.

I wish I could:

_____

_____

_____

_____

## THOUGHT PROVOKERS

### For Individual Reflection and Group Discussion

1. Imagine you are in the studio audience at a talk show when the authors of *The Caring Question* are being interviewed. You are asked to give them feedback about your perception of health and the single person. What do you say?

• How do you describe your life as a single? What has been the toughest aspect of being single that you've had to deal with? What has been the most freeing?

• What about the four traps of singleness? Have you fallen prey to their dangers? How have you escaped their clutches? What other perils and pitfalls have you encountered?

Make notes of those issues on which you want to speak your piece.

Compare your stories, feelings, and insights with others in the studio audience (your group or family or select friends). What common denominators do you find?

2. How do you feel about your place in the church as a single? What is the church's official response to you? In what ways is this response helpful? In what ways is it not helpful? What kind of reception do you receive from the people in your church? What's the prevailing attitude towards singles?

Remember—Jesus was a single adult!

- Do you think the local church understands and accepts this fact? What evidence do you have for your answer? How could you reach out with care to help others better understand the needs of singles in their midst?
- Do you think Jesus, as a single adult, faced what you face? In what ways specifically yes, and in what ways no? What did Jesus do about setting up his life-style as a single in the midst of a family-oriented culture? In what ways did he reach out beyond himself to others?

3. Make a list of both the special difficulties and rewards of reaching outside yourself as a single.

- What have you tried? With what level of success?
- What have you found most rewarding?
- What "reach-out" mission project might you try next?

# 11

# The Two Become One
## Reach Out to Your Spouse

Are you married? Oh, congratulations! How did it happen? For many, it happened like this:

One day while walking down the sidewalk of life you bumped into your dream. One thing led to another and before long you decided to walk life together. Before you knew it, there you were solemnly promising, in front of all your family and friends, "To have and to hold, for better and for worse, for richer or poorer, in sickness and in health, 'til death." The knot was tied, and the two of you became one. In the blink of an eye you made a lifelong commitment of staggering proportions. So far, so good.

But, there's one part we forgot. You also expected to live happily ever after. Well, we won't say this "happily ever after" can't happen, but we can tell you we've never met the couple able to pull off that part. Marriage as a lifelong relationship usually doesn't go quite that smoothly. It usually doesn't take couples long to find out that two don't become one without some rough spots.

Sure, before you got married you talked about how you would manage your lives together. But after the ceremony you had to figure out for real a few "minor" details like:

- Who balances the checkbook?
- Will we first buy a new couch or a motorcycle? Who decides?
- Who will shop? Cook? Carry out garbage?
- What will we eat? When?
- Who cuts the grass? Paints the house? Fills the car?
- How clean must the house be? Who cleans it?
- Where can I pile my stuff?
- Can I use your hairbrush? Your toothbrush?
- Who writes letters to parents? Or invites friends to dinner?
- Will the bedroom windows be open or closed?
- What bedcovers will we use?
- Will we squeeze the toothpaste from the end or in the middle?
- When we're together, who drives the car?

If you got through these questions, you tackled the next set of issues:

- How much time can I spend with old friends? Which friends? When?
- Whose family will we visit at Christmas?
- Can I go to school if I want to?
- Shall we have children? When? How many? Who will care for them?
- What shall we do for fun? When? With whom?
- Which church shall we join? How active shall we be?
- Will we have family devotions? Who leads prayers?
- Must we go to bed at the same time? What if I'm not tired?
- Can I shout at you when I'm angry? Can I sulk? Can I throw things, or throw up?
- Who initiates lovemaking? In what ways? What if I have a headache?
- Whose career is primary? When? Why?

In the weeks and months after the wedding, every couple is confronted with a landslide of questions like these that need to be answered. You probably assumed that you knew the answers. So did your spouse. You probably also knew you'd have to negotiate, but likely assumed you could negotiate *your* way.

If your expectations coincide with those of your spouse, there's no problem. When they differ, watch out! Misunderstandings, hurt feelings, and anger are just around the corner, and the "happily ever after" suddenly may not be very happy, and you may no longer be so sure it's forever.

At this point in a marriage you roll up your sleeves and get down to work. Marriages are not made in heaven. They don't just happen. People make them happen by the choices and sacrifices they make over the years to work out their differences. Marriages that last are based on hard work and a large measure of caring commitment.

*Think about your own relationship for a minute. How did you decide on the "minor" practical details of building a life together? How did you answer your questions? How did you weather the difficult moments?*

There is simply no way that people can share life together without periods of conflict. Individuals grow at their own rate and develop interests according to their personal internal pacing. This pattern makes it impossible for two people to go through life handcuffed together without some herky-jerky movement, some stumbling and a bit of chafing at the wrists, if not elsewhere. Sometimes your needs won't be met. Sometimes your partner's won't. Sometimes the feelings of love will evaporate temporarily. Fortunately, love is not a feeling, it's a commitment—a commitment

157

to reach out, even when you don't feel like it. This decision to love doesn't depend on the other person's response; it's a choice on your part. Like all commitments, marriage involves self-sacrifice as well as taking the risk to love with no guaranteed outcome.

Commitment provides the glue for a relationship that holds you and your spouse together when your relationship seems way out of balance. Marriage is based on continued hard work. It requires a constant process of clarifying and renegotiating the commitments we make to one another. It's not as if we can decide once and for all, "This is my commitment to you." Mutual understanding about how this commitment is to be carried out needs regular revision.

## COMMITMENT AT THE CRISIS POINTS

What happens when life together isn't so "happily ever after"? Most marriages have periodic struggles and crises that threaten the commitment partners have made to each other. Both people may be bitterly angry or unhappy. One partner may feel the enormous sacrifices aren't worth the meager rewards. One person may grow outside the relationship and feel exploited and discounted within it. The qualities of your mate that once attracted you may gradually become distasteful or threatening.

Marriage reaches a real crisis point when one or both partners actively consider leaving the relationship. At this point couples have two choices. First, they can choose to stick it out and work to resolve the crisis. Some couples decide to stick together no matter what the consequences. For those whose stubbornness leads in the end to a positive loving relationship, this choice is a wise one.

Second, couples can choose to end their mutual commitment and split. For some who have exhausted the possibilities for reconciliation, this may be the only decision possible. Others discover after uncoupling that their relationship was salvageable, and they wish they had worked harder to preserve their marriage. When does genuine commitment cross the line into self-destruction? Unfortunately it's impossible to tell for sure when you're in the midst of the struggle.

We do know that most people these days don't get much encouragement from their friends to work through the difficult times. The most frequent response is, "You'll have to take care of yourself. Do whatever will make you happy." While this may sometimes be cogent advice, we believe that couples should not split until they each have spent a good deal of time reviewing their commitment in the light of the following questions.

---

### Eight Questions to Ask Before You Split

- How am I contributing to the current crisis?
- What problems will I take with me when I split that are likely to resurface in other relationships?
- Am I willing to consider my spouse's well-being as important to me?
- If my partner's limitations were in some other area of life (for example, physical disability) would I be more tolerant?
- What would have to change for us to renew our commitment?
- Is splitting the only solution?
- Have we exhausted all potential resources for resolution and reconciliation?
- Could I learn what I need to learn from this situation without actually leaving?

---

Your answers to these questions may help you clarify what decisions you need to make in response to the crisis.

## STRENGTHENING YOUR MARRIAGE COMMITMENT

But whether troubled or not, all marriages need continued attention. Over the years we've found some tools that can help couples nurture one another and strengthen the life they've developed together. We've outlined three strategies for enhancing the health of marriages and the health of couples who choose to stay committed to each other. If you're interested in some friendly advice for strengthening your marriage relationship, these ideas are worth testing.

### REGULARLY RENEW YOUR COVENANT

The Old Testament uses the word *covenant* to describe the special promises and commitments that bind husband and wife together. We like to use this word when talking about marriage, since it suggests depth, permanence, dialog, and the wholeness we've been discussing.

By *covenant* we mean more than agreements about who walks the dog and how towels get folded. The promises implicit in covenant include cherishing one another, respecting one another fully, putting the other's welfare ahead of one's own, forgiveness, and the choice to love that transcends the day-to-day inconveniences, petty annoyances, and disappointments of living under the same roof year after year.

We rarely take the time—and the risk—of exploring and affirming this deeper level of relationship. We listen to the chatter of life around us, but how often do we *really listen* to the heart and soul of our partner? How often do you turn your ears on and focus exclusively on trying to know and understand your partner fully?

In what ways have you and your partner affirmed and adapted your marriage covenant over the past few years? How could you make the process of nurturing your commitment more intentional and meaningful? The Annual Covenant Renewal Format might make a good starting place.

---

### Annual Covenant Renewal Format

*Review the year in private.* Think about the past year in your marriage. What have been some of the joys, the highlights of your relationship? What about disappointments or frustrations? What do you particularly appreciate about your spouse and your commitment to one another? Identify those areas you'd like to affirm and those you'd like to adjust.

*Remember your covenant.* What promises did you make to your partner at the time you were married? Constant faith? Abiding love? Obedience? In what ways has your life this year affirmed those commitments? Have the two of you added to your covenant over the years? A forgiveness clause? Or a pact to share your feelings honestly with one another? How have you been doing in these special commitments? Write down your responses to these issues.

*Share your responses.* Spend time in a quiet setting where you can't be interrupted reaching out to your partner with your observations and hopes. Share what's deep in your heart. Listen with loving care. Be sure to tell each other directly what you most appreciate about your relationship. If there are areas of disagreement or disappointment, try to work out a mutual agreement for the future. If any issues cause pain or anger, table them for later. This is an opportunity for affirmation.

*Make it an annual ritual.* Find a way to publicly renew your covenant. How about an anniversary celebration? Involve your children, your parents, your friends. Hold a quiet ceremony at home or in church. Celebrate with joy your care for each other within the context of your wider network of support.

---

## KEEP IN TOUCH WITH EACH OTHER

The key to the health of any loving relationship is communication. Marriage is no exception. If you want to maintain a strong and vibrant relationship over the years, you need to talk with each other regularly and openly about your commitment and the issues that affect it. Marriage requires attention and maintenance to weather life's storms. Listening and sharing in a positive caring atmosphere enhances the health-fullness of both parties.

Most of us get caught up in the day-to-day trivia of our busy life-styles and find we have difficulty sandwiching in time for couple talk. It's easy to get lost in the crush of maintenance-oriented discussions chronicling the week ahead or today's triumphs and hassles while neglecting our time for nurturing one another.

Marriage and family therapist Mim Pew suggested to us this simple format for loving conversation. We tried it ourselves, with some skepticism, and discovered a wonderful process for getting in touch with ourselves and reaching out to one another. It's called a 30/30, and to reap its benefits you'll need to set aside one full hour for uninterrupted reflection and sharing. Don't let the formality scare you. The rules are important, so don't cheat on them!

---

### 30/30 Sharing Plan

*Make the appointment.* Agree on a time and place, preferably a day or two in advance, for 60 minutes of uninterrupted communication. Once this is decided, partners are on their own to keep the appointment—no "friendly" reminders or nagging or worrying. While you're at it, set up a time and place for the second 30/30 as well.

*Decide who will start.* One person will need to be the first sharer in this exercise. Flip a coin or decide by consensus on who will start first this time. Next time the other partner will get the first chance.

*Pick your topic.* If you're trying to resolve a difficult issue or share your feelings on a painful subject, identify the focus for the 30/30 and then table the topic until the time you've agreed on.

*Meet at the appointed hour.* Each partner is responsible for keeping the appointment at the proper place and hour. Locate yourselves so that you can't see each other's bodily posture or nonverbal expressions. The key to the 30/30 is communication without feedback. We like to do this exercise in bed, in the car, sitting back to back, or in a darkened room.

*Start sharing.* The beginning partner starts sharing at the agreed time. You can talk about the issue or whatever comes to mind. Share thoughts, feelings, opinions, attitudes, intentions, dreams, experiences. Periodic silence often deepens the level of communication. The sharing continues for 30 minutes while the other partner listens only and says nothing.

*Switch roles.* After *exactly* 30 minutes the second person starts sharing while the other remains silent. Again, you can talk about feelings, thoughts, or opinions. You can respond to what your partner has said or just head in your own direction.

*Let go.* At the end of this second 30 minutes both partners leave the scene. The subject matter of the 30/30 is not to be discussed until the next 30/30—at least 24 hours later—when the opposite partner begins the sharing.

---

## ACCEPT THE LIMITS OF YOUR RELATIONSHIP

Every relationship has areas of chronic trouble. They're called *chronic* because that's what they are.

They just won't go away, and you're faced with the need to accept them. Rather than continue to ask, "How can I get rid of this?" or "How can I change my spouse?" you might be better off asking, "How can I learn to live with this difficulty?"

It's not so awful to experience chronic problems. They may be painful, but pain is a part of life. They may cause you to be lonely, but it's possible to live with some loneliness. It's OK to have a less-than-perfect relationship! Too many people get trapped into ending a good thing just because it's not perfect.

The chronic problems in your relationship may limit you, but they don't define you. You are more than your problems. They may limit your relationship, but they don't define it. Your relationship is more than its problems. Don't let the pain eat away at the solid foundation. You can love yourself, and you can love your partner—despite chronic problems. Don't sell yourself a bill of goods. You do not have to be perfect to be loved. Your relationship does not have to be perfect to be loving.

Both your personal depth and the strength of your commitment are enhanced by your toughest thorns. You do grow and mature in response to difficulties. Every problem is a teacher. Allow those difficulties that won't go away to be your instructors for life.

## THE GIVING/GETTING RATIO

Like all commitments, "hanging in there" over the years requires self-denial and self-sacrifice. At some points your own self-fulfillment will be curtailed, at least in the short run. From our hours of listening to couples over the years it's become clear to us that marriage is not always a 50-50 proposition. Much of the time it's an 80-20 affair, with partners alternating the responsibility for energy investment. In some relationships the 80-20 is always weighted in the same direction. During some periods, especially in crises, one of you may be giving 100 percent while the other is unwilling, or unable, to give much at all. At other times your relationship may be 35-35 with both of you investing less than your fair share. Occasionally you may find that both of you pour your heart and soul into your relationship at an 80-80 clip. The lifelong commitment of marriage provides the security for times when you're out of joint with each other and the giving/getting ratio is way out of balance.

Marriage gives us a structure for self-sacrifice in depth. Marriages that work are based on the choices made over the years to reach out and care for each other's welfare whatever the cost.

## REFLECTIONS

Please take a few minutes to reflect on the outreach you make in your marriage.

---

### Personal Reflection on My Outreach to Spouse

Attitude toward my spouse (care, respect, ways of handling conflict, concern for spouse's lifelong development)

---

---

Communication patterns (frequency and quality of our time together, affirmation of what I appreciate, clarity of our mutual covenant)

---

---

Sacrifice of myself (what I invest or give up, the limits I impose on myself, the times I invest more than my share)

_____

_____

Chronic problems to accept (recurring trouble spots, disappointments, things I wish were different but probably won't ever change)

_____

_____

### Wish List for Health-Fullness

List here everything you can imagine wanting for a health-full commitment to your spouse. What would you like to be able to *do*? To *know*? To *feel*? To *learn*? Let your imagination run free. Don't limit yourself in any way. The wishes don't have to be practical. Have fun dreaming.

I wish I could:

_____

_____

_____

_____

## THOUGHT PROVOKERS

### For Individual Reflection and Group Discussion

1. Describe your honeymoon to some friends. Use slides or photos to illustrate your adventures, if you can. Embellish the stories as you tell them, expanding on both the disasters and the joys of that memorable period. Don't be afraid to laugh at your foibles. Then think through your early marriage again. Make notes as you look back on those years.

- When did the "honeymoon" end?

- When did the "happily ever after" start to change for you?
- What experience(s) confronted you with the change?
- How did you deal with your disappointment that all was not perfect?
- What steps did you take to roll up your sleeves and get to work on building a mature and loving posthoneymoon marriage?

Share your answers and experiences with your group or with someone you know who is contemplating marriage.

2. Your marriage commitment carries a cost and a reward. Complete the following sentences:

Because of my commitment to my spouse, I cannot _____, and I probably will never be able to _____, and I choose to _____ _____, in spite of some of my wishes.

Because of my commitment to my spouse I have received _____. I am stronger in _____, and my life is filled with rewards I would otherwise never have known such as _____, _____, _____, and _____.

Now put yourself in your spouse's shoes and complete the sentences again as you imagine he or she might.

- Share your answers with your spouse using the 30/30 format suggested in this chapter.
- Or exchange papers and spend 15 minutes together brainstorming the strengths and rewards of your relationship.

3. What is your assessment of the giving/getting ratios that have characterized your marriage over years? (50/50, 80/20, 30/30, 80/80, etc.)

- In the beginning _____
- Along the way (when?)_____
- At crisis points (which?)_____
- Today _____
- Next year _____
- Ten years from now _____

Explain your answers. Check with your spouse to find out if he or she sees it the same way.

4. Design a covenant-renewal process and ritual for your congregation.

# 12

# Who Is My Neighbor?

## Reach Out to People Around You

The family is the closest context for reaching out to care for others, but our commitments to outreach must go much further than the boundaries of our family. In the Christian tradition believers are called to love and serve their "neighbors" as one of the paths to health and wholeness.

Who is your "neighbor"? Family? Certainly. Friends? Of course. Colleagues at work? Sure. Strangers at church? I suppose so. Hungry refugees? Uh . . . . Hostile young punks? Well . . . . The disciples asked Jesus the same question, "Who is my neighbor?" His reply, "Anyone who needs you."

We've looked at the two-way dynamic of relationships within the family circle. The same principles of health-full give and take, of satisfying self-sacrifice, of rewarding commitment and cleansing compassion apply to our relationships with friends and "neighbors" as well. We believe that health-fullness is enhanced by a commitment to caring for others that focuses on the giving rather than the receiving and repeatedly chooses to reach out in love to whichever "neighbor" needs us at the moment. Consider this story by Roy Popkin:

## NIGHT WATCH

A nurse took the tired, anxious serviceman to the bedside. "Your son is here," she said to the old man. She had to repeat the words several times before the patient's eyes opened. Heavily sedated because of the pain of his heart attack, he dimly saw the young man in the Marine Corps uniform standing outside the oxygen tent. He reached out his hand. The Marine wrapped his toughened fingers around the old man's limp ones, squeezing a message of love and encouragement. The nurse brought a chair so the Marine could sit alongside the bed.

Nights are long in hospitals, but all through the night the young Marine sat there in the poorly lighted ward, holding the old man's hand and offering words of hope and strength. Occasionally, the nurse suggested that the Marine move away and rest a while. He refused.

Whenever the nurse came into the ward, the Marine was there, oblivious of her and the night noises of the hospital, the clanking of the oxygen tank, the laughter of night-staff members exchanging greetings, the cries and moans of other patients. Now and then she heard him say a few gentle words. The dying man said nothing, only held tightly to his son most of the night.

Along toward dawn, the patient died. The Marine placed on the bed the lifeless hand he had been holding and went to tell the nurse. While she did what she had to, he waited. Finally, she returned. She started to offer words of sympathy, but the Marine interrupted her.

"Who was that man?" he asked.

The nurse was startled. "I thought he was your father," she answered.

"No, he wasn't," the Marine replied. "I never saw him before in my life."

"Then why didn't you say something when I took you to him?"

"I knew right off there had been a mistake, but I also knew he needed his son, and his son just wasn't here. When I realized he was too sick to tell whether or not I was his son, I knew how much he needed me."

People need people. The young Marine knew this eternal truth. Like a good Samaritan in modern uniform he saw his neighbor's need and responded to it with compassion, concern, and commitment. What the young man may not have comprehended was that his act of reaching out was probably as health-full for him as it was satisfying to the dying old man. Relationships are the vehicles of healing for both the giver and the receiver.

In order to be truly healthy we must reach out— outside ourselves. Make friends. Give support. Pay attention to the needs of others. Encourage others to take care of themselves. Whenever we offer acceptance, love, forgiveness, or a quiet word of hope, we offer health. When we share each other's burdens and joys, we become channels of healing. No matter how timid or tired or selfish or crazy or young or old we are, we all have something important to offer each other.

*How about you? When you're at your very best, what is it that you offer others? With whom do you share that healing gift? What do you receive in return?*

## YOUR CARING IS ESSENTIAL

Your "neighbors" need your support and care. To offer yourself is a choice you alone can make. Love is a decision, not a feeling. If you want to promote love, live like a lover. You can choose to reach out and touch someone—many someones! Break beyond your boundaries and give yourself to others. They need you.

The investment will take energy. Your focus on others may at times drain you. It will certainly take time from your private pursuits. You'll risk rebuff and rejection. You'll experience loss and grief when neighbors you have loved die or go away. The rewards are uncertain. But it's worth the risk. You can't be truly health-full in isolation. Reach out. Choose to love.

You can make a difference in your world by reaching out—with your attitudes, with your heart, with your hands, with your imagination, with thanksgiving. When you reach out with care and commitment, you heal both yourself and your neighbors.

Where do you start? With your attitude.

## REACH OUT WITH YOUR ATTITUDE

Reaching out can be a risky business. When you commit yourself to loving your neighbor in general, you never know when a particular neighbor is going to pop up with a need you can fill. It takes an attitude of openness and curiosity to leave your personal circle of security and step across invisible boundaries into the unknown.

It's not too hard to offer your services to an elderly neighbor whose lawn needs mowing. Or to a friend who needs a ride to the dentist. You may gladly volunteer for a PTA committee or cancel a movie date to spend the evening visiting an acquaintance who's hospitalized. The risk of reaching out to people in our own circle is minimal. But most of us draw that circle quite tightly around ourselves and thereby close ourselves off from a world full of neighbors.

Think of the last party you went to, or church potluck, or school meeting. Which people did you include in your reach-out circle? Which did you ignore or interact with only superficially? For most of us the second group is by far the larger.

What about all the people you know only by face—salespeople, old folks, shopkeepers, airline attendants, bus drivers? Are you businesslike and formal with them, or even rude when they don't jump to meet your needs?

We often make our judgments about others based on very little information—physical appearance, the tone of voice, clothing, age. We decide this person is a snob. That one is spacy. Another is a rigid conservative. We draw the circle that includes some and excludes others. Have you ever been thrown into a new context with someone you had previously locked out of your circle and soon discovered, much to your surprise, that as you got to know them they were intriguing? And your opinion changed to let them in? At that moment your neighborhood was enlarged with just a simple change in attitude!

The real test of our capacity to reach out in a health-enhancing manner comes when we consider the people we tend to write off and write out of our lives—the "undesirables," the "unloved," the "forgotten." Most of us structure our lives so that we aren't confronted by the needs of these creatures of God who make us uncomfortable, who evoke from us an involuntary shudder or nervous laugh. Yet these people also are the neighbors we are called to serve.

*How about you? Which type of people never or rarely feel the healing touch of your care for them? People with physical defects? A different skin color? A strange language? Someone with mental limitations? The ill? Queer people? Weird people? Old people? Fragile-looking people? What about the disoriented, the deaf, or the "crazy"? Do you avoid religious fanat-*

*ics or people who are less capable than you? How about folks with dirty hands or warts on their noses or braces on their legs? What neighbors are still waiting for you to risk caring about them?*

The call to service and self-sacrifice challenges us to respect and respond to the humanness of each person, from bosom buddy to Bowery bum. People who reach out regularly evidence a deep respect for others as people. They offer an outlook of positive expectation to strangers as well as friends, to check-out clerks as well as colleagues, to waitresses as well as tennis partners.

Compassion and gentleness in day-to-day living requires that an attitude of openness, curiosity, and caring pervade all human contact. It's these attitudes coupled with the willingness to risk that allows you to walk across a room, stick out your hand, and say, "Hi, I know we've met before, but I can't remember your name. Help me out. I'd like to try again!"

---

### Attitude-Stretching Exercise

Think about your week ahead and the people you're likely to make contact with—at work, shopping, church, meetings, concerts, the Y. Choose one person you would usually brush past or greet only perfunctorily—a bank teller, a construction worker, your principal, a crochety neighbor, the blind woman who rides your bus, the Vietnam vet in the next office.

Focus on that person now for a minute. Open your mind and consider what that individual might be like as a human being. What needs might this neighbor be carrying that you could meet? What might brighten the day for this person? What could you do to reach out?

Resolve to reach out and make positive contact with this neighbor at your next opportunity. Use some of the ideas in the rest of this chapter. See what happens.

Work to expand this attitude of openness to more and more people.

---

## REACH OUT WITH YOUR EARS AND HEART

The most valuable skill for reaching out to others is the art of listening with your heart. This gift of listening deeply and carefully to the concerns and feelings of another person is called empathy.

*Empathy* literally means to "feel in"—to stand in another's shoes for a moment, to get inside another person's feelings. Through this process of tuning in to another's feelings and responding in a way that confirms you have heard, you can show understanding and acceptance. Everyone needs empathy. No matter how successful or discouraged or confident or lonely we are, all of us ache to be understood fully.

Look around at the signals your neighbors are sending. What about the troublemaker in your son's homeroom? Do you suppose he could be saying, "No one knows how I feel. No one cares."? What about the person who pushes ahead of you in the line at the post office. Is it possible she needs someone to listen to the pain in her life? What about your colleague who's always putting other people down. Could she really be asking, "Please, someone understand me!"

*What about you? When in your life have you really wanted to be heard? Who has listened?*

Empathy seems deceptively simple. All you have to do is listen. Yet most people find it very difficult to "merely" understand and acknowledge another's feelings. It doesn't feel like we're doing anything. When we hear the cries of our needy neighbors, it's tempting to try to fix the problem and remove their pain rather than accept, understand, and support them. So we give advice. We ask questions. We share our experiences. We diagnose the problem. We focus on *our* solutions, *our* opinions, *our* viewpoints. And we miss the key, for the key to empathy is keeping our focus on the other person rather than on ourselves.

Empathy is hard work. You have to pay attention— yes, *pay!* It costs something when you choose to tune in to someone else. It takes time, energy, and the willingness to focus on meeting the other's needs rather than your own. Empathy begins with the difficult decision to pay this price. The next four steps are a little easier.

**Listen actively for feelings.** Notice all the cues. Words account for only 35 percent of all communication. What feeling clues do you get from nonverbal messages, gestures, facial expressions, postures? What feelings might be reflected in the tone of voice? Tune in with all your senses. Soak up the feelings.

**Clarify anything you don't understand.** Ask questions. Encourage further explanation. Empathy requires heart-felt caring, an attitude of genuine interest in the other person.

**Acknowledge the feelings you hear.** It's not enough to think you understand your neighbor. You need to respond in such a way that other people know their feelings have been heard and understood. Restate the feelings you heard in your own words to check the accuracy of your understanding.

**Affirm the other.** To listen empathically is to understand your neighbor's feelings and accept them as true, even if you don't feel the same way, even if you don't think they're appropriate, even if the feelings upset you.

Sharing, understanding, and accepting of feelings is the heart of human relationships. Empathy is the skill that activates these processes between people and allows people to give themselves to each other.

*What about you? When was the last time you gave
your attention as a gift to someone and really listened
closely, with empathy? What gets in the way of your
really hearing and accepting others? Think back over
today. What bad listening habits prevented you from
reaching out? Fear of yourself? Wanting to fix the
problem? Being afraid of the feelings, or not agreeing
with them? Asking too many questions? Giving advice? Focusing on your own problems? Wanting to
be liked?*

True listening is rare. It is a gift of yourself you
can give to another. God gave us two eyes to see with,
two ears to hear with, two nostrils to smell with, and
two hands to touch with—but only one mouth! Maybe
we should use our mouth only one-ninth of the time!
At least we should listen twice as much as we talk.

How could you practice listening more fully? With
what neighbors will you start? Reach out and touch
someone with your eyes, your ears, and your heart.
Show you care—*listen!*


## REACH OUT WITH YOUR HANDS

Reach out and touch someone—really *touch* someone. Does that suggestion raise the hair on the back
of your neck? Frighten you? Perhaps even excite you?
As we were growing up, most of us learned to keep
our hands to ourselves and not invade other people's
space. We learned our lesson so well that when we
bump into someone in a crowded elevator we say
"Excuse me," rather than "You're welcome!" In this
society we keep our distance.

How sad! Physical contact is one of life's richest
blessings—a powerful means of communication and a
largely neglected health-giving resource. A Colorado
orthopedic surgeon trains ski patrol members in what

he considers the most important emergency-care technique—touch! From the moment of first contact on the slope until arrival at the hospital, teams are instructed to be sure that one member always maintains caring physical contact with the injured skier. It's been shown that skiers brought in by these teams fare significantly better than others. Broken legs and collarbones set more easily and heal more quickly when touching is an integral part of the treatment.

Scientists have been measuring the importance of touch for several decades. In his famous experiments with monkeys Harry Harlow determined that "contact clinging is the primary variable that binds mother to infant and infant to mother." Another study by Patton and Gardner demonstrated that children deprived of a close maternal relationship showed disturbed mental and physical growth. The bonding of infant to parent seems dependent on touch.

Touch is important in more casual relationships too. In a recent research project at a university library, the clerk contrived to touch every second person who checked out a book. Outside the building investigators asked students their opinions of library services. The group of students who had been touched was significantly more satisfied. In a fourth study a woman stood at a pay phone, fumbling through her purse for change. She explained her plight to all passersby who noticed. Those whom she touched on the arm while she talked were more than twice as likely to offer her a dime as were those she spoke to without making physical contact. Touch is a powerful way to reach out.

A college instructor from Brainerd, Minnesota, has gained quite a reputation in our area as the "mad hugger." He breaks all the "rules" about touching in our culture. He hugs anyone and everyone he meets.

Some think he's a bit odd, but in the process he offers a lot of warmth and energy to others. Why not become a mad hugger yourself? Some people may be surprised at first, but if you practice it often enough, your neighbors will soon figure out you're for real. Don't be surprised if they start hanging around you, waiting for more of the same.

*How do you feel when people touch you? How much is physical closeness and touching a regular part of your daily life outside the family? What are your "rules" about touching? Who needs to be touched by you today?*

Positive, caring physical contact lets the high energy juices flow between people, filling each person with vigor and vitality. You can hardly touch without being touched in return. You have a marvelous health-giving resource at the end of your arms and many touch-hungry neighbors waiting for physical strokes. Initiate a health-enhancing exchange. Make sure that touch is a part of every contact you make.

## REACH OUT WITH THANKS-GIVING

A little appreciation goes a long, long way. Studies have shown that gratitude is a more powerful motivator than money. Most of us will really put ourselves out just to hear someone say thank you.

When a friend or a stranger reaches out to you, returning the gift in kind is rarely necessary. Usually a simple sign that you appreciate the kindness will be gift enough. Gratitude is a way of reaching out in return.

*How do you feel when someone tells you directly how much they appreciate you? In what ways do you reach out to others by showing gratitude? In what ways are you careless about remembering to demon-*

*strate your appreciation? Who needs to hear a thank you from you today?*

If you want to improve your thanks-giving style, you could try one or more of the suggestions below.

**Get in the habit of giving thanks.** Say it directly. "Thank you for your warm smile!" "I appreciate the energy you contributed to this meeting." "Your thoughtfulness made me feel so loved. Thanks again!"

**Practice your attitude of gratitude.** Actively look for actions and qualities in others that you appreciate. If you liked the attitude of your waitress, tell her so. If the play moved you, let the director know. If your friend's advice was helpful, tell him even if it means losing face.

**Form a mutual-admiration group.** If some people in your life don't like to give and receive appreciation, find some who do and spend time with them.

**Select small, unique gifts that carry a personal message from your heart.** Surprise people with them. Gifts you create—poems, notes, wall hangings—speak most clearly.

**Once again, get into the habit of thanks-giving.** Say it directly! "Thanks for listening to me." "You're always so positive—thanks!" "Knowing you care keeps me going."

## REACH OUT WITH IMAGINATION AND SPONTANEITY

The trick in reaching out is to train yourself to notice others' needs and then be ready to share your gifts when they are appropriate. We should volunteer, not out of economic necessity or because of budget cutbacks, but out of our own need to give to the neighbors around us. Check with your church and local voluntary-action center for suggestions on where your services might be most useful. If you or they run out of ideas, try several of these:

## 26 Outreach Options

- Be a foster grandparent.
- Counsel at a camp for handicapped kids.
- Provide a listening ear for hospice patients.
- Act as chauffeur for kids with working parents.
- Share your talents and knowledge with nursing-home residents.
- Invite a foreign student to spend time with your family.
- Sit with a stranger in church and listen empathically afterwards.
- Pick up group-home residents to share in a family outing.
- Visit regularly at a jail or prison.
- Find a job for a refugee.
- Deliver meals on wheels.
- Donate blood regularly.
- Supervise the playground during lunch periods.
- Adopt a grandparent in your neighborhood.
- Assist with health screenings.
- Relieve parents of a chronically ill child.
- Stop for a stranded motorist.
- Take a loaf of bread to a bereaved neighbor, even if you don't know her well.
- Open your home to victims of a disaster.
- Fund a week at camp for a needy child.
- Talk to the shopping-bag lady outside the library.
- Support your local Boys' Club or Girl Scouts with time as well as money.
- Telephone someone you know is lonely.
- Transport seniors to the store or appointments.
- Give back rubs at a day-care center.
- Write cards and letters frequently to folks who need their spirits lifted.

Be prepared. You never know when your neighbor might need you. Where you see the need, step in like the Marine. Whenever you reach out to another, your own health is enhanced along with the well-being of the person who receives your care and concern.

## REFLECTIONS

Before we move on to consider your outreach to creation, please take a few minutes to reflect on your patterns of reaching out to your neighbors. Do your outreach habits enhance or erode your health-fullness?

### Personal Reflection on My Outreach to Neighbors

My attitude toward people (judgments, inclusion/exclusion, types of people)

_____

_____

My listening skills (willingness, hearing feelings, "fix-it" mentality)

_____

_____

My use of touch (how? when? to whom?)

_____

_____

My actions of gratitude (compliments, thanks, gifts)

_____

_____

### Wish List for Health-Fullness

List here everything you can imagine wanting in your outreach to others. What would you like to be able to *do*? To *feel*? Let your imagination run free. Don't limit yourself in any way. The wishes don't have to be practical.

I wish I could:

_____

_____

_____

## THOUGHT PROVOKERS

### For Individual Reflection and Group Discussion

1. Draw the "circles of your neighborhood." Here's how:

Take a blank sheet of paper. Start by drawing a small circle for self and family in the middle of the paper.

Next draw a bigger circle around "self" for your friends. List all the friends you can think of—old friends and new ones, ones who live near and far. Mentally go through your Christmas card list.

Next draw a still bigger circle for acquaintances. Include school parents, service people, church members. List everyone you can think of in the time you have. Include names if you know them. Make the outside edge of this circle very heavy and bold.

Finally, outside your circle at the edge of your paper, list all the people who are currently excluded from your reach-out circle. People you don't like, of different ages or different styles, "undesirables" to you, forgotten, institutionalized people in homes, jails, or hospitals, people who make you uncomfortable, people of different ethnic groups, evangelists, humanists, physically defective people, weird people, fragile people, etc.

Choose one person from each of your "neighborhood circles" (outside your circle, acquaintances, friends) and consider how you would go about moving them one step closer to you in your "neighborhood." Make the outreach contact you imagine and see what happens.

2. Hug—or in some other way physically touch—the next three people you speak to. Yes, no matter where you are or who you're with! No matter what the circumstances. Touch them! See what happens. If you're with people you trust, talk about what you just did and share your reactions.

3. Check out your local newspaper. Read all the articles, features, ads, classifieds. As you read each, ask yourself, "What is needed here? Who needs my caring? How could I reach out?" Make a list of the needs you discover just from creatively reading the paper. Don't stop with less than 100! Choose one of these local needs and plan a strategy for reaching out to the person(s). Put your plan into action and report back to your group.

# 13

# **Tackling the Issues**
Reach Out to Your World

We've drawn the caring circle around family, friends, and "neighbors." The next step toward a healthy balance involves reaching out with compassion and concern for the "things" of creation and the people beyond our "neighborhood" of personal contact.

We need to explore some difficult and challenging questions about our responsibility for protecting God's creation—from saving electricity to saving the seals to saving the children. This, too, is part of our outreach.

## REACHING OUT TO THE WORLD

If we want to be truly health-full, we can't limit our reaching out to family, friends, and "neighbors" close at hand. We need to view ourselves as citizens of the worldwide community, called to responsibility for the causes and concerns of all creation. What an awesome undertaking! How does one start looking after the world? It's somewhat like eating an elephant: you just take one bite at a time.

The task begins with commitment. Remember the three principles of making commitments in relationships? Choice, sacrifice, and risk taking are essential elements of our investment in causes as well. We start with choices, simple day-to-day choices about where we invest ourselves. These choices add up over time to create a solid commitment.

South African Alan Paton, author of *Cry, the Beloved Country,* prominent spokesman for equality and justice, did not set out to be a crusader. Until age 40 he was a reform-school administrator with little public visibility. In his writing he responded, however, to the cries of injustice he saw around him, and he spoke eloquently of the human cost of apartheid. As he matured, his moral commitments grew with him. Without seeking the role, he became an intellectual and spiritual leader loved the world over but kept under surveillance in his own country.

A little closer to home, a friend of ours, Andy, started by talking to a wheelchair-bound classmate. Casual conversation led to genuine concern about the obstacles she faced in her effort to lead a normal life. Soon he was launched on a full-scale investigation into the needs of those unable to walk. Eventually Andy organized a student-interest group that lobbied effectively with the school board to allocate funds for several small changes that made life much easier for the handicapped students at his school. Andy went on to study architecture and now specializes in designing structures that enhance the lives of people with physical disabilities. A career of outreach and service began with a brief conversation and grew slowly over time with increasing levels of commitment.

Julie's decision to boycott a major food producer started with a movie at church about infant malnutrition in the Third World. Dave and Lynn first learned

about world hunger from a student distributing leaf-
lets at the state fair. What they heard appalled them.
Now they dine one night a week on the average diet
of many of the less fortunate—one cup of rice—and
send the money they save to Bread for the World.

The Swansons took in a runaway for the weekend
and discovered new purpose in life. Now they're part
of a network of treatment homes for adolescents who
desperately need loving structure.

All these people found new meaning and fuller
health when they took the first small step and reached
out to make a difference in their world. How do we
decide where to invest ourselves? It's tough! We have
only a certain amount of personal resources—time,
energy, and finances. The needs of creation are overwhelming. Should we tackle sudden infant death or
job discrimination or illiteracy or juvenile delinquency
or violence on TV or violence between nations? Even
if we do, will our efforts make any difference? Should
we contribute to the Salvation Army? Public radio?
Planned Parenthood? Cancer research? Foreign mis-
sions? Which causes truly deserve our attention and
investment? It's a question of personal choice.

*What about you? What human problems concern
you most these days? Where have you chosen to commit yourself and your resources? What small steps
have you taken already? Start with the needs evident
right in your own backyard and see where they lead
you.*

## THE COST OF REACHING OUT

Commitment also implies sacrifice. When you
choose to invest your time or money in a cause or concern outside yourself, the choice leaves less time and
money to spend on yourself and your needs. If you
decide to invest more time and energy in the effort to

regulate nuclear waste disposal, you'll have to rearrange your priorities and sacrifice somewhere—maybe less time with the family or less briefcase work at home in the evenings, perhaps dropping out of the bowling league or choir for a while. Grabbing on to a new cause usually means letting go somewhere else.

A dentist we know takes a month of vacation in the summer. So do many others. But Dr. Drinkwater is different. He packs his van full of dental supplies and equipment and heads for rural Mexico, where he wanders the backroads offering dental care to all who need it, free of charge. He considers this commitment his fair share in making the world a better place for others. Although he works harder that month than he ever does at home, he always returns refreshed and renewed for another year. Physicians and nurses who volunteer for assignments in Cambodia or Peru or Sudan feel this same commitment to reaching out. So do Peace Corps or VISTA volunteers. They all sacrifice time and financial rewards in favor of having a positive impact on the world by helping those in need.

*What about you? What sacrifices do you make in order to reach out to creation? What might you have to give up in order to invest more deeply in some cause or issue?*

The risk factor of commitment is especially high when we reach out to the world beyond our immediate community. We can never know ahead of time whether our sacrifice will make the difference we hope.

The Carpenters came back from a trip to Seoul determined to offer a better life to at least one starving child. After two years of delay and red tape, a five-year-old orphan arrived from Korea to join their family. Vic and Louise threw themselves into the project of integrating Christopher into their life. Nine months later it was clear that all their love and concern and commitment and prayers were not enough. Christopher was still unable to speak more than a few words, and his needs were consuming nearly all the family energy. Louise and Vic had to face their own limitations and the reality of the situation, including the needs of their three other children. The adoption agency found a new home for Christopher, and the Carpenters grieved the loss of a son and brother.

The results of reaching out were not as Louise and Vic had hoped and dreamed. But that fact doesn't diminish their outreach and commitment one whit. The value of commitment can't be measured by the success or failure of the project we've invested in. The only real gauge of commitment is our own assessment of how much we have invested ourselves.

*What about you? Have you invested yourself in some cause or issue that didn't turn out as you had hoped? How do you feel about these "lost" causes?*

## TRANSFORMING PRINCIPLES TO ACTION

We've heard the stories now of several people who felt a commitment to a principle and then turned their concern into action. Where do you start? How can you choose to relate to your world with compassion and a vision of the interconnectedness of all creation?

**Start with your attitude.** As with reaching out to your family or your neighbors, attitude is the key. If you've focused primarily on grabbing for yourself as much of this world's goods as you can, as fast as you can, you'll never reach out. Perhaps you recall TV images from the 1960s of riot-torn cities, looters running, arms loaded with merchandise. Obviously, these folks were in no mood to slow down and help injured neighbors nearby. To do so would have required them to let go of "their" goods.

Most of us certainly aren't stealing others' treasures. But if we're focused entirely on filling our arms with as much of this world's merchandise as we can get and then carrying it with us through life, we also won't be able to reach out and help very much.

Having enough to satisfy your needs is important, but how much is enough? Too many possessions tend to complicate and clutter life, clouding its deeper purposes and values. The focus on gathering as much money and material goods as possible is not a worthy purpose for life, and its pursuit will keep you too busy to reach out. You'll have to decide when enough is enough.

A prime requirement for readying yourself to reach out to your world may be the willlingness to voluntarily choose a more simple pattern of living. Simplicity does not necessarily mean returning to a more primitive style. Most people are aware of the distractions and unnecessary complications that clutter their lives. Simplicity means unburdening yourself from those awkward distractions and learning again to live lightly in a voluntary simplification and reduction of needs.

Simplicity is not a turning away from progress, not a withdrawal from the world, not an escape to rural living. The simplicity we are talking about occurs right where you live at this moment. It unfolds as you challenge your present life-style.

*How about you? In what ways is your life unnecessarily complicated? What elements of compassion are missing in your life because of your cumbersome possessions? Are your consumption patterns basically satisfying, or do you buy much that serves no real need? In what ways could you improve your life by simplifying it?*

Setting limits for yourself and deciding when

enough is enough will allow you to focus some of your attention on outreach rather than solely on personal accumulation. The willingness to live more simply will help you learn to relate to your world gently, to walk through life lightly, leaving as few marks on creation as possible. An attitude of simplicity can open for you the opportunity to find a new quality of depth in your relationships with things, with your world, with your neighbors, and with yourself.

**Expand your consciousness.** Open your eyes to the world around you and notice the problems and issues that call for response. Continue to educate yourself about issues and potential avenues for commitment. Read the newspaper with an eye for concerns that might merit your involvement. Take in TV specials on national or world issues. Find out where your local and national church bodies are investing their efforts and funds. Go to speeches and demonstrations. Talk to others about their personal commitments to wider concerns. Read your "junk" mail. Subscribe to a newsletter that keeps you posted on pending legislation at the national and state levels. Your local library is a good resource for pamphlets and information on topics of concern. If you're still looking for a cause, try one of those suggested in the Outreach Catalog below.

---

## Outreach Catalog

*Human rights:* Freedom, peace, justice, world hunger, poverty, freedom of speech, right to life, equal rights, equal employment opportunities, civil rights, anticommunism, pacifism, migrant workers' conditions, apartheid, nonviolence.

*Ecological concerns:* Litter, air pollution, water pollution, urban renewal, endangered species, overpopulation, wild rivers, national parks, strip mining, nuclear power, nuclear wastes, acid rain.

*Health:* Medical research, health care facilities, anti-smoking, prohibition of alcohol, health care around the world, drug control, health screening, black lung disease, Agent Orange, consumer rights, malnutrition, drug education, contraceptive education.

*Handicapped:* Barrier-free access, special olympics, rehabilitation, group homes, socialization programs, adoption, humane treatment for the mentally ill or retarded.

*Education:* Literacy around the world, higher education, arts in the schools, gifted education, special education, UNICEF, tutoring, A Better Chance.

*Family:* Family violence, right to life, sexual assault, disaster relief, support for bereaved families, crisis shelter, parenting education.

*Aging:* Health care, fixed incomes, housing standards, nursing home care standards, crime protection.

*Community:* Courtroom monitoring, correspondence with prisoners, voter registration, political caucus or convention, temporary foster care, charitable groups, rehabilitation of juvenile offenders, citizen advocacy.

Check yourself out. Read through this list of causes one by one and decide to which ones you've made a mental or philosophical commitment. Then go back and mark those concerns where you've acted on your principles by reaching out.

---

**Narrow your focus.** Once you've explored the options for outreach, you need to target your investments. Decide what issues or needs you will isolate for action this year (or month or week). *What are your priorities? Which issues concern you the most? Where do you imagine you can have the biggest impact? Do you want to focus on local or national or international concerns?* Narrow down the possibilities. Be sure to explore at least one new project as well as the old favorites.

**Move into action.** Now you're ready to design a

strategy. Decide how much time, energy, and money you're willing to spend in your total outreach efforts. Then draw up a plan. You may want to throw yourself wholeheartedly into a single concern such as air pollution or energy conservation. Or you may want to spread your efforts around. Some issues may merit large financial investment. Others may require substantial time commitment. Decide what would be a healthy and health-full balance for you.

Transforming your attitudes into behavior is the key to healthful outreach. It's easy to say you value freedom of speech; it's tougher to march in protest when that right is violated or to sit in courtrooms monitoring trials. It's tougher, but more rewarding, when you back up your principles with action. There are numerous ways to get active. Not everyone is a marcher or a good public speaker. The trick is to find the cause and the role that fits your interests and abilities.

As you plan your strategy, bear in mind the wide variety of ways you might implement your commitment. Here are some ways to get going:

- *Research the issue.* Find out everything you can about the subject.
- *Write letters.* The written word is powerful.
- *Speak up.* Don't be shy about saying what you think.
- *Sticker your bumper.* Display your colors on your car.
- *Pound the pavement.* Canvass/solicit door-to-door.
- *Let your fingers do the walking.* The phone makes efficient, effective contact.
- *Use visible symbols.* Arm bands and flags speak silently but clearly.
- *Join an organization.* There's camaraderie and potency in numbers.
- *Boycott.* Offenders listen when you hit them in the pocketbook.

- *Hike or bike.* Your sponsors and you might even enjoy it.
- *Donate used articles.* What you no longer need may be useful to others.
- *Reach for your wallet.* No cause ever has enough money.
- *Open your home.* This is an age-old refuge for troubles and troubled.
- *Pray.* Open your heart to the power beyond you.

Plan to reach out however you like, but take the first difficult step and get started. Then see where it leads you.

## REACH OUT FOR HEALTH

Have you noticed that the healthiest, most vital people around are also alert to situations in which they can help? They're always reaching out, looking for opportunities to care for their world. They've discovered a secret many of us miss. The gift we give comes back to us—multiplied.

Jesse Summit is a good example. He built much of his life around reaching out beyond family and "neighbors" to support people and causes. He took three years out of a successful career to join a government service project in an underdeveloped country. In his retirement he continues the active pattern of his working days, now volunteering his administrative skills to help small businesses get on their feet or untangle their management messes. Jesse's active at church and serves on the boards of several nonprofit human-service organizations including United Way and the community mental health center. He still finds time to record books for the blind and to visit and write regularly to former business associates in nursing homes. Jesse supports numerous local, national, and international organizations with generous financial contributions. Few people know the extent of this gentle man's outreach to the world. But Jesse Summit knows. He knows the reward of caring for creation and the wealth of health he receives in return.

Do you think Jesse is too good to be true? No, he's just a plain person like the rest of us who years ago made a decision that outreach would always be part of his life. And he's carried on that commitment throughout his whole life.

People all around us live their lives that way. They may be hard to discover, since they never talk about what they do. They store within them the richness and warmth of their giving.

When you reach out with care and concern for your world, you open yourself to the healing experience of unity with all creation. It's an experience impossible to know when you're locked inside your own home caring only for your own. We need to listen to the world in the pains of birth, groaning toward that great day when harmony will prevail. The sacred in our world and in our hearts will come alive only as we reach out beyond ourselves and the boundaries of our own immediate desires, when we see ourselves as part of the whole of creation, when we commit our energies to making a positive difference in our wider world.

Healthy people are aware of and concerned about the world beyond family and neighborhood. We believe it is health-enhancing to sense and accept our responsibility to care for the world's resources and its inhabitants. These concerns and causes deepen our experience and provide the kind of meaning that makes life worthwhile.

Reach out to your world like Jesse Summit. The gift of health-fullness you receive in return will be priceless.

# REFLECTIONS

Before we move on to consider the caring question from its widest perspective, please take a few minutes to reflect on your pattern of reaching out to the world. Do your reach-out habits in this area enhance or erode your health-fullness? How do your habits affect the things and people of creation?

---

## Personal Reflection on My Outreach to Creation

Attitude toward things (consumption style, usefulness vs. beauty, clutter in life)

_____

_____

Life-style (cooperate or compete with nature, voluntary simplicity)

_____

_____

Commitment to principles (social justice, human rights, education)

_____

_____

Investment of time, energy, and resources in caring for creation (actions supporting causes and concerns)

_____

_____

## Wish List for Health-Fullness

List here everything you can imagine wanting for a health-full attitude toward creation. What would you like to be able to *do*? To *know*? To *feel*? To *learn*? Let your imagination run free. Don't limit yourself in any way. The wishes don't have to be practical. Have fun dreaming.

I wish I could:

_____

_____

_____

_____

## THOUGHT PROVOKERS
### For Individual Reflection and Group Discussion

1. Go through your checkbook and make a list of everything you spent money for in the past 30 days. Divide the items and services you purchased into two columns:

| Purchases that increased the quality of my life, the lives of others, and that of my world | Purchases that complicated my life and/or decreased the quality of life for others and for my world |
|---|---|

What do you observe about your spending patterns and the quality of your life? What changes would simplify your life? Share your insights with others in your group.

Make an inventory list of everything in your house (or at least in one room). Do it just as the furniture movers do when they arrive with the van. Divide your possessions into two lists:

| Items that enhance the quality of my life and that of others | Items that detract from my life and complicate it for me and others |
|---|---|

What do you observe about your accumulation of things? What changes would allow you to reach out to your world with more energy and greater clarity?

2. Make a list of what you consider to be the moral issues of your time—include international, national,

state, and local issues. Then ask yourself what you are doing to respond to each in a manner that fits your beliefs and priorities.

3. Write down the name of a person, like Jesse Summit, who reaches out to his or her world as an *unsung hero or heroine*. You may think of a person you've known or one you've only read about, someone who's alive or dead: Martin Luther King, Mahatma Gandhi, Dag Hammarskjöld, Florence Nightingale, or someone as caring and principled from your own private circle.

Meditate on the qualities of this person for five minutes; then answer these questions:

- What is his character? Her focus?
- What makes him or her so special? So admirable?
- In what ways would you like to emulate this person?
- What would be a first step you could take?

Compare heroes and heroines with others in your group. Then for the next week, take a poll on unsung heroes and heroines. Ask everyone you meet about his or hers. Keep track of all the suggestions and report back to your group.

4. What would the world be like now if the disciples of Jesus had all gone back to fishing, tax collecting, and doctoring rather than trying to change the world?

- How did their commitments change their own lives?
- What if you were to do the same thing? Where would you start? How would your life change?

# PART 3
# BALANCE

# 14

# You First or Me First?

## The Caring Question Revisited

So there you have it—the caring question, "Me first or you first?" You can't be healthy unless you care for yourself. You aren't healthy unless you put your health to use for others.

On the one hand, health-fullness requires self-care—taking the best possible care of God's gift to you—body, mind, spirit—with all your strengths and limitations, potentials and frailties. On the other hand, you can't be truly healthy without reaching out in service to meet the needs of others—making contact, bearing another's burdens, listening to cries of pain or despair or anxiety, protecting your environment. When one aspect of health is pursued and worshiped as if it were the whole, the balance is upset and health-fullness is forfeited.

This balance may look easy on paper, but it's never easy to practice. Why? Because there are no clear rules for determining when to take care of yourself and when to take care of someone else.

# THE INTERNAL DIALOG

For example, how do you answer these questions? "Do you have a right to take care of yourself? A responsibility?" Most people quickly answer yes, but in their hearts whisper no. The conversation goes something like this:

Yes, I have a right to take care of me because I'm worth it.

> No, I don't have a right, at least not right now, because it would be selfish.

Yes, I'm the only one who really knows what I need.

> No, others need care more than I do.

Yes, I'm the temple of God's Holy Spirit.

> No, it's better to give than to receive.

Yes, I must, or soon I won't be able to care for me or anyone else.

> No, others would be angry and disappointed in me.

Which side gets the last word in your dialog? How often do you say, "Me first"?

The other-care side of the balance raises parallel questions. Do you have a responsibility to take care of others? A right? "Of course," you say. But again, your internal dialog clouds the issue.

Yes, I am called to be a servant. To sacrifice myself for others is the greatest good.

> No, I've got to look out for myself.

Yes, I feel more worthwhile when I see that I've helped someone else.

No, after all, the world's dog-eat-dog, everybody's on his own. If I don't protect myself, who will? Your job is to take care of you. My job is to take care of me.

Yes, I made a commitment to care and no matter what it costs me, I will stick it out and keep my side of the bargain.

No, I must grow and fulfill myself, and unfortunately right now, reaching out to you would hold me back.

Which side gets the last word here? How often do you say, "You first, I'll wait"?

The healthy balance is excruciatingly difficult to put into practice because at every moment you must ask the caring questions, "Is now the time to take care of me? Or of you?" When and under what circumstances do you neglect your own needs to take care of others first? How do you decide?

It would be much more comfortable to latch on to one set of answers and relieve ourselves of the decision-making dilemma. "Others first," once and for all. Or "me first" from now on. The conflict would be minimized, but in the process you'd lose the balance.

The balance decisions are made even more difficult because we live in a culture ruled by conflicting ideologies. Our society was founded on a "duty ethic" that focused on other-care. Today the personal self-fulfillment ethic with its theme, "Take care of yourself," has risen to equal status. The two currently compete for our loyalty.

# CULTURAL MESSAGES: THE DUTY ETHIC

Thirty years ago Americans recouped from the Depression and the war years and settled into a life-style characterized by earning a living, raising your family, doing your duty, and living responsibly within the "God-given" rules of society. Women lived out their assigned roles as homebodies, and men went out to work at winning the bread and bringing home the bacon.

The duty ethic remains very much a part of our culture. Which of us hasn't been influenced, who hasn't been infected by one of these mottoes: "It's better to give than to receive," "Do unto others," "Work your fingers to the bone," "Give your all to (a) your family, (b) the company, (c) your church, or (d) the cause"? We've learned from childhood that pleasing others is of primary importance, pleasing parents, pleasing teachers, pleasing neighbors, pleasing everyone—except yourself.

The keynote to this life approach is self-sacrifice, a value that is exemplified by the Christian tradition of service to others. Unfortunately, at its extreme this ideal may tip the balance toward self-neglect, when the call to serve gets improperly translated as, "Deny yourself at all costs," or "Always put others first." We see people pursuing wholeness through martyrdom, sacrificing their own needs and waiting expectantly for others to notice their caring and return the favor. Martyrs abdicate responsibility for their own well-being, expecting others to bestow health upon them. As loving and altruistic as this type of self-sacrifice may seem, it's a tragic trap. You cannot receive from others a gift you're unwilling to give to yourself. Health-fullness requires personal self-care as well.

The selfless duty-to-others path to health seems to ignore the "as thyself" part of the "love your neighbor" passage. If you give and give and give, what happens when you near the bottom of the pot? Do you go on giving less and less to more and more? Even the most dedicated saints need to refuel periodically by taking good care of themselves.

## CULTURAL MESSAGES:
## THE SELF-FULFILLMENT ETHIC

The current generation set out to improve on the recipe for the good life based solely on other-care. We saw and rejected the results of the duty ethic at its extreme. Having experienced the greatest expanse of affluence in our country's history, we asked, "Is this all there is?" And we set out on a search for a better way than our parents had known. We sought meaning through freedom and self-fulfillment without limits. We were hungry to experience everything, to live life for the moment, to become independent, mature, fully developed individuals free from the constraints of cultural rules or responsibility to others.

Ours was the luxury of personal freedom and choice. "Make of yourself whatever you will." "Do whatever feels good." "Anything goes." "Don't stifle your growth." "Be sure to look out for #1," we were told, and we set out to get what we wanted!

No longer did women have to stay home and have babies, nor did men have to be the providers. No longer were there set rules on how to be "man" or "woman." No longer was sexual intercourse confined to the marriage bed. No longer did we stay in relationships that confined us and curtailed our individual chances for growth. Only one rule remained, "Develop yourself to the fullest of your individual potential!" Self-fulfillment became your sacred responsibility and yours alone—to follow your own private path and take good care of yourself.

Unfortunately, in its extreme form this ethic has not brought us full health either. Researchers report that the adolescents who grew up in the 1960s and who are now approaching middle age are haunted by frustration, anxiety, and depression.

The freedom to "do as you please, when you please, if you please" all too often becomes the freedom to "do your own thing all by yourself." It's not uncommon for those who have tested all that life has to offer to feel lonely, empty, void of purpose and direction. Stymied and immobilized by the multitude of choices, they ask wearily the old question once more, "Is this all there is?"

## THE TWO ETHICS

Research by Daniel Yankelovich indicates that approximately 20 percent of Americans are relatively untouched by the "me first" ethic of this generation. They live out their lives firmly rooted in the ethic of duty to others. On the other hand, 17 percent of Americans live a life-style primarily characterized by the extremes of the self-fulfillment ethic. That leaves a vast majority of us, 63 percent, caught in the middle, firmly committed to carrying out all our responsibilities to others while still cherishing the dream that we can be free to develop in whatever way we choose, whenever we choose.

How about you? Which cultural ethic do you tend to buy into? The quiz below will give you some indication.

You may wonder what some of the questions have to do with other-care and self-care. But each item raises a characteristic that distinguishes those in the two extremes, so answer the questions and see how you fare. Choose one statement in each pair.

# The Two Ethics Quiz

| A | B |
|---|---|
| _____ I feel a strong need for new experiences and I seek them out. | _____ I would like to feel secure before I try anything new. |
| _____ Satisfaction comes from personal growth and shaping my own life freely. | _____ Satisfaction comes from investing in a permanent home and family life. |
| _____ A woman should seek to fulfill herself independently as her first priority. | _____ A woman should put her husband and children ahead of her career. |
| _____ I would seek psychotherapy (counseling) willingly. | _____ I would not seek psychotherapy willingly. |
| _____ I prefer to be creative (enjoy taking risks). | _____ I prefer to be financially secure. |
| _____ I like to try new foods and tastes. | _____ I would rather eat what I already know I like. |
| _____ I believe children should be brought up to think for themselves and make their own decisions and mistakes. | _____ I believe that children should have clear rules—old-fashioned discipline is better and clearer for them. |
| _____ I believe premarital sex between consenting adults is fine. | _____ I believe premarital sex is wrong. |
| _____ I believe that work must be meaningful —or shouldn't be done. | _____ I believe work must be done whether I enjoy it or not. |
| _____ I believe that you can't trust the | _____ I believe our government in |

American government to make moral decisions.

_____ I believe it's just as healthy and acceptable to remain unmarried as to marry.

_____ I hate either/or questions and didn't answer them all—the rules you set up made me angry.

Washington is doing what is right and can be trusted.

_____ I believe that there's something wrong with an unmarried person who chooses to remain single.

_____ Some questions were difficult but I could answer them all without getting upset.

Total _____          Total _____

## HOW TO INTERPRET YOUR SCORE

The statements in Column A are indicative of the self-fulfillment ethic. Column B statements characterize the believers in self-sacrifice. If you checked 10 or more statements in Column A, it's probable that you're in the 17 percent who find themselves living out the extreme of the self-fulfillment ethic. It's also likely that you periodically experience the dead-end traps of "going it alone."

If you checked 10 or more statements in the self-sacrifice column, you're likely to be among the 20 percent of Americans untouched by the "me first" ethic. You probably put others' needs ahead of your own and tend to diminish your health by neglecting your own self-nurture.

If you checked a maximum of 7, 8, or 9 items in your preferred column, you're among the vast majority of Americans caught in the middle between two conflicting world views. You clearly incorporate some of the principles of each ethic within your beliefs.

# REFLECTION

Do your personal beliefs more closely match those of the "duty to others" ethic or those of the self-fulfillment approach? How do your beliefs get translated into action? Have you been spending yourself in a balance of self-care and other-care that's health-full for you?

Stop and reflect on your answers to the caring question. Review the insights you've gained and the notes you've made as you worked through this book. Then use the instructions and circles below to record your observations.

---

### Personal Reflection on My Healthy Balance

Imagine that the space within the circle below represents all of your available time and energy. Consider the ratio between the amount of your time and attention you currently focus on self-care and the amount you focus on other-care. Then divide the circle into two pieces that represent this ratio and label each segment. Of course, you can't be absolutely sure, so just make the best estimate you can.

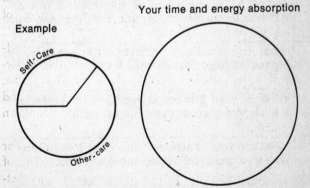

Your time and energy absorption

Example

Self-Care

Other-care

Next, using dotted lines, divide your self-care portion into pieces that accurately represent your current time and energy investment in the four aspects of self-care: physical, mental, relational, and spiritual. In the same way divide the other-care portion into pieces that accurately represent your current investment in the four aspects of other-care: family, spouse, neighbors, and causes. Label each of the eight pieces.

**Your time and energy absorption**

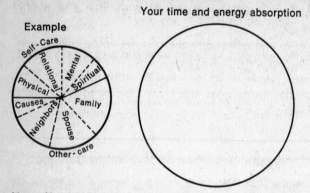

**Example**

*Note:* If you don't have any idea how you're spending your time and energy these days, keep track of your activities for a week; then come back and complete this exercise.

1. Look at your self-care/other-care balance. How do you feel about your healthy balance as represented by your division of this circle? Will this balance be sustaining for you over the long run?

_____

2. What is your primary commitment in self-care, the biggest slice of the self-care pie?

_____

3. What is your primary commitment in other-care, the biggest slice of the other-care pie?

_____

4. What are your reactions? How does this picture fit with your personal values and priorities?

_____

5. What is your smallest self-care slice?

_____

6. What is your smallest other-care slice?

7. What are your reactions? How does this picture fit with your personal values and priorities?

8. Would you like to adjust your time and energy spending patterns in any way?

9. Would you like to increase the size of any investments? Which ones?

10. Which slice or slices would you be willing to reduce in order to reinvest more in your priorities?

Don't cheat here! Be honest. When you increase your commitment in one area, you'll have to decrease it in another. If you're unwilling to cut anything out, you're not only fooling yourself, but also setting yourself up for failure.

## THE LIMITS OF TIME

Clearly it's tough to make healthy balance decisions because life presents us with more options than we can ever pursue. It's all too easy to get caught in the illusion that we can take care of all others' needs while fully caring for our own at the same time. We can't. The limits of our time and energy force us to compromise, to make choices.

You alone can decide what to do with your time and energy, but never can you respond to every opportunity in your path. Your choices to spend yourself are forced choices. When you spend yourself in one way, you necessarily must neglect other options.

You have time to do exactly what you choose to do. You can't make more time. You can't squeeze more time. You can't save time. You can only spend it—in more or less health-full patterns.

## INTERNAL WISDOM

The only way to spend your time and energy wisely is to know clearly the goals and purposes for which you live and then to make your decisions accordingly. If your purpose in life is to prove you can make it on your own, your self/other-care choices will be quite different from someone whose purpose in life is to please others or to bring about world peace. If you are deeply committed in your faith, your behavior will reflect your beliefs. If you don't know where you're headed in life, you're likely to squander your time and energy resources. Have the purposes that are absorbing your time and attention enhanced your health?

Unfortunately, most of us are only vaguely aware of the beliefs and goals that guide our decision making. In times of great crisis or pain such deeply rooted values come into sharp focus. Priorities suddenly become clear. We know for sure what's important in life and what's worth spending our time and energy on. It's difficult to feel the same clarity of goals and certainty of purpose in the humdrum or hustle-bustle of daily decisions. Yet the same wisdom and spiritual depth guide these decisions as well.

You don't have to wait for tragedy or death to illuminate your life and point the way to health-full choices. You can use the worksheet below to help you get in touch with your deepest life purposes and then proceed to live out your answers to the caring question.

## Purpose-in-Life Reflection

Is it appropriate for you to die?

Why or why not?

When is it appropriate to die?

At what age do you think it would be most appropriate for you to die?

Use the circle at right to represent the total number of years you feel it would be appropriate to live. Draw a line out from the center and label it with the proper age. Based on your current age, and the number of years you hope to live, calculate the percentage of your time you have already lived and the percentage that is still left.

Example

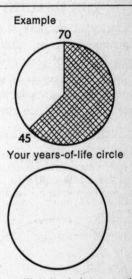

70

45

Your years-of-life circle

Divide the circle into two segments representing those two percentages. Shade the part of your life you have already lived.

Now focus on the time that is still left. Ask yourself: Why not die now?

What's left undone that I should do or be in the remaining time?

What should I do with the remaining time so that when

I reach my selected age, it will be appropriate for me to die—and I can look back over my life with no regrets?

_____

_____

In answering these questions you've begun to state your purpose in life. My purpose is:

_____

_____

_____

_____

## THE HEALTHY BALANCE IDEAL

Clarity of purpose and direction frees us to make adjustments in our time- and energy-spending patterns. In light of your new wisdom how would you like to balance the reaching in and reaching out aspects of your life? The worksheet below will help you identify your healthy balance goals.

---

### Healthy Balance Goals

Use the circle below to illustrate your healthy balance goals. From your current viewpoint, how would you like

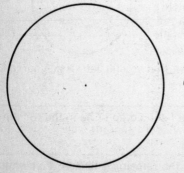

Your *desired* time and energy absorption

your circle divided for maximum health-fullness? First, indicate your desired self-care and other-care balance. Then divide the self-care section into physical, mental, relational, and spiritual slices. Divide the other-care segment to reflect your desired commitment to spouse, family, neighbors, and causes.

Compare your ideal healthy balance pie to the one you drew at the beginning of the chapter. What portions of the circle did you *leave the same,* indicating no change desired?

Self-care/other-care balance

_____

Individual self-care priorities

_____

Specific other-care priorities

_____

Congratulate yourself for those areas where you feel your investments are already healthy. Affirm for yourself that you're on the right track.

What portions of the circle did you *change or adjust?*
Self-care/other-care balance

_____

Individual self-care priorities

_____

Explain

_____

Specific other-care priorities

_____

Explain

_____

Which areas of the healthy balance do you most need to work on?

_____ self-care          _____ other-care

What specific aspects?

| _____ physical | _____ family |
| _____ mental | _____ spouse |
| _____ relational | _____ "neighbors" |
| _____ spiritual | _____ causes |

What general observations can you now make about your personal priorities and about your current healthy balance level? *I am:*

_____

_____

_____

Summarize the major adjustments in priorities you believe would be healthful for you over the long run. *I'd like to:*

_____

_____

_____

These could be used as your goals for change. Once you're clear about the specific adjustments you'd like to make in your own healthy balance, go back and read the relevant chapter(s), paying particular attention to the suggestions for change. Then start testing out some new involvements and see how they work for you.

---

## TWO FINAL CAUTIONS

**There are no absolute right answers.** This is not a recipe book. We cannot tell you exactly how to mix the ingredients to bring out the flavor you wish for your life. We've outlined the resources and principles for obtaining maximum health and wholeness, but the combinations will be your own unique approach. Your personal priorities may indicate that for you all aspects of health should not be balanced in equal proportions.

Keep on testing until you find the balance that works well for you. Over the years you'll keep adjusting and revising until you find a style that brings you the quality of life that you seek.

**You don't have to be perfect.** We have shared many ideas about physical, mental, relational, and spiritual self-care; then about family, spouse, "neighbors," and causes—other-care. Don't try to tackle all of them at once. Remember the issue is balance, and every change you make, no matter how small, can alter the balance in a health-full direction.

We can all tolerate minor imbalance. In fact, perfect adjustment is never possible. Life is unfair. It throws curves, and we lurch off balance. Pain, anger, loneliness, and struggle result. But the tension we experience from imbalance is tolerable.

Occasionally you may even purposefully choose to *create* imbalance. For example, you might stretch your physical limits and go without sleep for a time. Or you might reach out to others who need you, without an immediate full return. Relationships can be one-sided for a week, or a year, or many years. We all learn to live with reality, imperfection, and compromise. These often create an imbalance. That imbalance doesn't ruin our health, unless it remains too far out of line for too long a time.

So, get as clear as you can about what's important to you. Then move ahead boldly, making decisions with faith in the future and confidence in your ability to rebalance as necessary. Live within your personal limitations and just learn to be the best *you* you can be.


## A FINAL CHALLENGE

How by your choices do you carve out a life-style that takes responsibility to others seriously without neglecting yourself? How do you on the other hand invest in your own self-development without being seduced into the trap of trying to fulfill all your needs?

There are no easy formulas for investing in permanent relationships and causes for which you would die while also remaining responsive to the fulfillment of your own ever-changing feelings and needs.

As tough as the task is, we encourage you to seek your health-fullness in the meeting ground between the two—to find a livable and deeply satisfying balance between your responsibility to yourself and your responsibility to others.

Your answers to the caring questions will always reflect that continual struggle for balance between self-care and caring for others.

Balance is not a noun. It's never a static condition we can preserve. Balance is a verb, a process we engage in over and over again. Move *beyond wellness* by keeping your life in a healthy balance.

## THOUGHT PROVOKERS

### For Individual Reflection and Group Discussion

1. Write out your personal dialog in response to these questions:

- Do you have a *right* to take care of yourself?
- Do you have a *responsibility* to take care of yourself?

YES, because ...        NO, because ...

_____   _____

_____   _____

_____   _____

_____   _____

Pair up with someone and read your conversations out loud, with one person taking the *yes* role, the other the *no* role. Feel free to improvise as you go.

If you're in a group, generate your list together and put it on a blackboard or newsprint. You may want to use only Bible passages or biblical stories to support both sides of the argument.

Talk about the process and your personal dialogs.
- How do you decide when to care for you and when others?
- What's your typical pattern? How often do you decide one way or the other?
- In what specific situations do you always say no or always say yes?

2. Complete the healthy-balance assessment and planning process outlined in this chapter.
- Share your observations and insights with others.
- Listen to their answers. Compare notes.
- Be sure to respect each other's individual priorities and choices.

3. Make a health report card for each person in your group or family. Using an index card for each person, list the three positive health habits you admire in that person (optimistic attitude, service in the community, intensity of feeling, empathy, etc.). Then go around the group telling each person directly the qualities you appreciate, giving specific examples of health-full behavior you have observed. After each person has given and received appreciation from every member, sign each person's report card and give it to him or her with a wish for continued health-fullness.

---

Donald A. Tubesing and Nancy Loving Tubesing provide consultation and continuing education seminars in a wide variety of business and human service settings. For further information, please contact them at:

**Whole Person Associates, Inc.**
**P.O. Box 3151**
**Duluth, MN 55803**
**(218) 728-4077**